Public Broadcasting Foundation of Northwest Ohio

A young mother pauses to sing "The Song That Never Ends" with her child.

A Businessman, who is hard-of-hearing, utilizes the closed captions on the Newshour with Jim Lehrer.

A retiree remembers the smell of Tiedtke's Department Store.

A soul is stirred by the near-perfect digital sound of a symphony.

A young cook is instilled with the bravery to try a new recipe for the first time.

For over 30 years WGTE Public Broadcasting has added flavor and seasoning to the lives of its viewers and listeners.

What's Good To Eat:

The Best of Northwest Ohio

Toledo Farmers' Market

WGTE Public Broadcasting

Special
Edition

Regional Planning Committee

Donna Niehous, Chair
Fran Anderson, Maumee
Dino Brownson, Perrysburg
Faye Fenwick, Toledo
Pat Frechette, Toledo
Jennifer Hester, Sylvania
Irene Kaufman, Toledo
Suzanne Petti, Findlay
Frazier Reams, Perrysburg
Yanula Stathulis, Toledo
Kathy Steadman, Toledo
By West, Toledo
Sandy Wisely, Toledo

Victoria M. Souder, Chairman
WGTE Board of Trustees

Cover photography by Jim Weyer, Weyer International Inc.
Cover design by Dave Jablonski
Photographs by Joanna Backlund and Tom Paine
Food photographs by Jim Weyer

International Park on the Maumee
River, East Toledo

Noisettes Of Pork Tenderloin with
Root Vegetables in Puff Pasta
Served in a Honey Dijon Mustard
Espagnole Sauce
by Chef John D. Wesley
J.D. Wesley's Bistro
5333 Monroe Street
Toledo, Ohio 43623
See Page 84

Appetizers

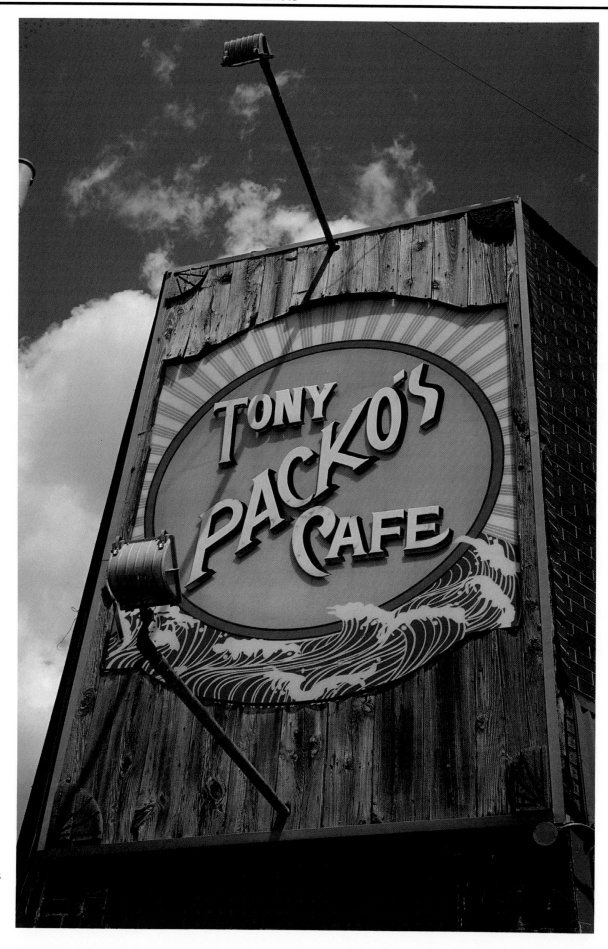

World Famous
Tony Packo's
Cafe
See Page 115

Historic Weber
Building, East
Toledo

Italian Hors d'oeuvres

1	package fresh basil leaves
8	ounces cream cheese
3 or 4	ounces goat cheese
1	container pesto
1	package sun-dried tomatoes

Line a 5 or 6 inch bowl with plastic wrap. Make a design on the bottom of the bowl with the basil leaves. Mix the cream cheese with the goat cheese. Drain the pesto. Snip the sun-dried tomatoes. Layer the cheese mixture in the bottom of the bowl. Next, layer the pesto, and then cover with the sun-dried tomatoes. The last layer should be the cheese mixture again. Refrigerate overnight. Invert on a plate. Serve with crackers. Cut out one wedge to show the Italian colors. Decorate plate with basil leaves.

Tortilla Roll-ups

6	large flour tortillas
2	8-ounce packages cream cheese
1	can green chilies, drained
1	can small black olives, drained
1	can small pimentos, drained
1	package Hidden Valley ranch dressing

Combine all the ingredients except the tortillas. Spread the mixture on the tortillas. Chill for 2 hours. Cut into strips, like jelly rolls. Serve with salsa.

Makes many appetizers for 12 to 15 people.

Italian French Stick

2	eggs, beaten
1	cup milk
1/4	cup oil
2	tablespoons sugar
1/2	cup grated Parmesan cheese
1 1/2	pounds ricotta cheese
1/2	pound diced pepperoni
1/2	pound diced salami
3	cups flour
1 1/2	teaspoons baking powder
1	teaspoon salt
2	tablespoons fennel seed
1/2	teaspoon baking soda
1	teaspoon black pepper

Mix together eggs, milk, oil, sugar and cheeses until blended. Coat meat with dry ingredients and stir into egg mixture until blended.

Spoon into greased double French breadstick tins.

Bake in 350° oven for 1 hour or until done. Cool 30 minutes before removing from pans and place on rack to finish cooling. Wrap in foil and refrigerate. Slice 1/2 inch thick. You may serve cold or at room temperature. The breadsticks also freeze well.

Makes two French sticks.

No-fuss Delectable Wine Punch

2	10-ounce packages frozen strawberries
2	10-ounce packages frozen lemonade
2	bottles rose wine
12	7-ounce bottles 7-Up
	fresh strawberries
	lemon

Mix all ingredients in blender. Depending on the size of the blender, the ingredients may have to be cut in half. Garnish with fresh mint sprigs, sliced fresh strawberries and thinly sliced lemon.

Makes 10 to 14 servings.

Brie with Sun-dried Tomato Topping

2	pounds brie
6	tablespoons parsley, minced
6	tablespoons Parmesan cheese, grated
10	sun-dried tomatoes, minced and packed in oil
3	tablespoons oil from the sun-dried tomatoes
12	cloves garlic, minced
3	tablespoons fresh basil
3	tablespoons chopped pine nuts

Chill brie well before handling. Combine the other ingredients. Remove the rind from the top of the brie. Spread topping. Place on microwaveable serving plate. Microwave about 60 seconds, or just long enough to soften the cheese.

Makes 12 to 15 settings.

Chicken Spread

1	5-ounce can Swanson Premium chunk white chicken, shred with fingers
1	8-ounce package cream cheese, softened
1	8-ounce carton sour cream
1	teaspoon lemon juice
1	teaspoon Worcestershire sauce
1	teaspoon garlic powder
1	tablespoons pickle relish, plus a little juice

Combine all the ingredients and chill for several hours. Serve on assorted crackers and breads.

The Renowned Toledo Museum of Art

Toledo Botanical Gardens

Baked Garlic Herb Spread

1 1/2-2	whole buds fresh garlic
2 to 3	tablespoons olive oil
1/3	cup fresh chives, chopped
1	pound soft margarine
1/4	cup fresh thyme, chopped
1/4	cup fresh parsley, chopped
1	tablespoon Luzianne Cajun spice

Peel the garlic bud and cut off the top of the bud. Try to ensure that some small part of the top of each clove is cut off. Place the garlic in a clay garlic baker (ideally) or in a piece of tin-foil shaped like a muffin cup. Pour the olive oil over the garlic buds, ensuring that the tops are especially coated, as well as the sides. Bake the garlic in a 350° oven for about 45 minutes. The garlic is done when it can be squeezed (after cooling) and a garlic paste flows out easily, like toothpaste from a tube. If the garlic is baked for too long, it will turn brown and become dry.

Squeeze the baked garlic into a sealable, plastic container. Use a fork to mush the garlic to a smooth consistency. Add the chopped herbs and seasoning mix. Mix thoroughly with a fork. Add the margarine and stir together again, thoroughly with a fork.

The resulting mixture should keep in the refrigerator for 3 to 4 weeks. It could probably also be kept in the freezer nicely, but seeing as we always use it quickly, we have never tried this.

Makes approximately 20 one-ounce servings.

Note: The herbs are just a suggestion. If you like fresh basil, oregano, cilantro or rosemary, feel free to pick and choose.

Cheese Ball

1	8-ounce package cream cheese, softened
1	5-ounce jar Kraft old English cheese
2	5-ounce jars Kraft Roka Blue cheese
	ground walnuts
1	teaspoon each:
	onion powder
	garlic powder
	lemon juice
	Worcestershire sauce
	dry mustard

Blend all ingredients and chill until firm. With lightly oiled hands, shape into 2 to 5 balls or logs. Roll each in ground walnuts. Wrap in plastic. Can be frozen. Serve on assorted crackers.

Christmas Punch

2	quarts cranberry juice
1	6-ounce can frozen lemonade concentrate, thawed
1/2	cup maraschino cherry juice
6	10-ounce bottles Sprite, well-chilled

Combine all ingredients. Serve over ice ring in punch bowl. Garnish with lemon slice, orange wedge, maraschino cherry alternated on cocktail picks.

Makes about 40-4 ounce servings.

Moot Punch

Wonderful for Christmas or St. Patrick's Day

6	ounce package lime gelatin
2	cups hot water
1/2-1	cup bottled lime juice
2	12-ounce cans frozen limeade concentrate (may substitute lemonade)
9	10-ounce bottle Sprite or 3 quart bottles
1	teaspoon almond extract
	Up to a fifth of vodka (optional)

Dissolve gelatin in hot water. Stir in frozen limeade. Add bottled lime juice. Pour over cracked ice or ice ring. Add Sprite. Add vodka, if desired. May garnish with fresh lime or lemon slices, if desired.

Makes 40-4 ounce servings.

Punch for Forty

1	cup crushed pineapple
4	cups sugar
2	quarts boiling water
	juice from 6 lemons
	juice from 6 oranges
1	quart grape juice
2	cups freshly made tea
1	quart carbonated water

Cook pineapple, sugar and water for 15 minutes. Add fruit juices and tea. Chill. One hour before serving, pour over cracked ice. Just before serving, add carbonated water.

Makes 3 or 4 gallons, enough to serve about 100 people.

Pupu's

(Hawaiian for appetizers)

1	cup mayonnaise, not salad dressing
2	tablespoons dehydrated minced onions, reconstituted
1	tablespoons parsley flakes
	sharp cheddar cheese

Mix and chill for several hours. Spread generously on Triscuits. Top with slices of sharp cheddar cheese. This can be done 2 to 3 hours before serving. When ready to serve, place under a broiler until the cheese is slightly melted. Serve immediately.

Allow 4 for each person.

17

Mary Alice Powell's Hidden Treasures

This fascinating appetizer is filled with surprises that hide under a savory topping. It gives the host a wide selection of munchies to hide, chosen according to season and the budget. In the summer it's nice to stick with vegetables only, but around holiday time, shrimp is a welcome treasure.

2	cups mayonnaise
1/2	cup sour cream
1/2	cup horseradish
2	teaspoons dry mustard
1/2	teaspoon salt
1	teaspoon lemon juice
	cucumber and green pepper squares, cherry tomatoes, canned mushrooms, water chestnuts, sautéed chicken livers and/or shrimp.

Combine mayonnaise with sour cream, horseradish, dry mustard, salt and lemon juice. Arrange vegetable and other choice of foods on the bottom of a serving dish. Spread dressing over the top to cover foods completely.

Serve with toothpicks to jab the goodies. If someone who gets a chicken liver doesn't like them, he can pass it on to another guest who does and dive again.

The original recipe called for monosodium glumate, but we all know that's a no-no.

Herbed Oyster Cracker Snacks

1	teaspoon garlic salt
1	tablespoon dill weed
1 1/2	cups oil
1	package dry ranch dressing
23	ounces oyster crackers

Put crackers in a large plastic bag or paper grocery sack. Pour combined ingredients over them. Shake the bag. Shake, shake, shake. Let stand overnight.

Elizabeth Barry's Marinated Chevre on Herb Toast with Tomatoes Balsamico

Elizabeth Barry owns The Ginger Jar in Perrysburg, Ohio

	chevre cheese
	dry bread crumbs
1/4	cup Ginger Jar Balsamic Vinaigrette
	crusty bread slices
	olive oil
	chopped, fresh herbs
	Roma or Plum tomatoes
	basil, chopped
	Greek olives

Roll little lumps of the cheese in the bread crumbs and set to marinate in 1/4 cup (or more) Balsamic Vinaigrette. Flip after 10 minute to moisten the other side.

Brush bread slices of bread with olive oil, toast in 300° oven for 3-4 minutes until golden. The toaster oven is fine for a few slices. Do the same for the other side, but spread a mixture of chopped fresh herbs before toasting.

Meanwhile, slice the tomatoes, splash with Balsamic Vinaigrette, strew with basil. Add olives if you have the strength to open the jar.

Microwave the cheese for 1 minute on high or until lightly melted and serve with the tomatoes and oil/herb toast.

Mushroom Paté from Judith Lodes of Lady Fingers

2	tablespoons butter
8	ounces mushrooms, cleaned and finely chopped
1 1/2	teaspoons finely chopped garlic
1/4	cup finely chopped, green onion (white only)
1/2	cup white wine
2	teaspoons chicken base
4	ounces cream cheese
1	teaspoon green onion tops, chopped
	salt and pepper to taste

Heat butter in medium skillet over high heat; add mushrooms, garlic, green onion, wine and chicken base. Cook until all liquid is evaporated. Let cool to room temperature.

When cool, add cream cheese and green onion tops; mix well. Salt and pepper to taste. Can be molded into a ball or ring mold or just spread on toast points or crackers or sliced French bread.

Artichoke Paté

1	can artichoke hearts, squeezed of excess water
2	cloves garlic, crushed
2	tablespoons white wine vinegar
1/2-2/3	cup olive oil
1/2	teaspoon salt
1/2	teaspoon sugar

Process artichokes, salt, sugar and garlic until finely chopped. Add the vinegar and continue processing. Add oil a few tablespoons at a time until it is all used and paté is fairly fine in texture.

This is good spread on toasted pita points, but it can also be stirred into pasta with butter and Parmesan. Use about 2/3 cup to a pound of pasta with 3 tablespoons butter and a half cup grated cheese.

Herbed Butter Popcorn

1/2	cup butter or margarine
2	tablespoons minced chives or onions
1/4	teaspoon thyme
1	teaspoon basil
1/4	teaspoon marjoram
1	teaspoon salt
4	quarts warm, unsalted popcorn

Melt butter, add seasonings and chives or onions. Heat very slowly to blend flavors, 8 to 10 minutes. Drizzle butter mixture over popped corn. Toss lightly to coat corn evenly.

Soups

Bleu Cabbage Soup

4	slices bacon, cut up
1	medium onion, diced
1/2	medium cabbage, sliced thin
1/4	teaspoon thyme
1/4	cup dry white wine
	pepper to taste
6	cups chicken broth, about 1 large can
4	ounces crumbled bleu cheese

Fry bacon in soup kettle, remove and drain. Keep about 2 tablespoons fat in pan, sauté onions. Add cabbage, wine, thyme and pepper. Cook about 5 minutes or until cabbage is tender. Add chicken broth, bring to a boil and simmer about 30 minutes. Serve soup in bowls, sprinkle with bleu cheese and bacon. As with all soup recipes, the measurements are approximate. Season to taste.

Makes 6 servings.

Golden Dragon Chicken Soup and Red Dragon Beef Soup

	a 3 1/2 quart or larger microwaveable bowl
1 1/2	quarts water
1	cup bok choy, leaves and stems, sliced and chopped
1/2	cup celery chopped
1/4	onion chopped
1	small can beef broth or 2 bouillion cubes
1/2	teaspoon dried parsley, or use fresh
8	ounces tomato sauce
1	cup rotini
	dash black pepper
7	ounces mushroom pieces, drained
	left over chopped roast beef

Golden Dragon Soup

	Ingredients are the same except:
	chicken broth, fat removed, instead of beef
	no tomato sauce
	Ramen oriental noodles instead of rotini

Cook carrots, bok choy, celery, onions and parsley in water for 20 to 25 minutes until tender. Add beef broth, tomato sauce and rotini. Cook until rotini is tender.

*The optional roast beef and mushroom pieces may be added after the vegetables are cooked, but before putting in the rotini.

Italian Wedding Soup

Meatballs

2	pounds ground beef
3/4	box 8-ounce Italian flavored bread crumbs
3	eggs, whipped with a wisk or a fork
1	tablespoon dried parsley flakes
1/4	cup grated Romano or Parmesan cheese
1 1/2	teaspoons salt
1/2	teaspoon pepper
1	teaspoon garlic powder
4 to 5	shakes Accent

Soup Base

8	quarts water
1	soup bone or 5 pieces beef stew cut into dice-size pieces, may also use turkey or chicken carcass, if so, substitute chicken cubes for beef bouillon cubes
1	medium carrot, sliced thin
2	large celery sticks, sliced
1/2	medium onion, sliced
4 to 5	shakes Accent
1/4	teaspoon dried parsley flakes
2 1/2	tablespoons salt
5	beef bouillon cubes
2	teaspoons chicken concentrate
1/2	tablespoon tomato sauce
1 1/2	pounds fresh escarole

For meatballs: Thoroughly mix all ingredients in bowl. Cover and let stand for two hours. (This is important.) Roll mixture into approximately 1/2 inch round balls. Pour a quarter to a half inch of oil in a frying pan and fry meatballs until well-browned. A deep fryer or Fry Baby may also be used. Makes approximately 180 half-inch meatballs.

Wash, trim and cut the escarole into small pieces. Do not use the very white center of the escarole head. It may be saved and used in salads. Put escarole into boiling water for 8 to 10 minutes, then drain and set aside.

For soup: Boil all ingredients in large pot on medium-high for 2 hours. If the soup is not to be frozen, put meatballs and escarole into soup base and cook for 45 minutes.

If the soup is to be frozen, freeze meatballs, escarole and broth separately. Before cooking, combine all three and cook for 45 minutes.

Makes approximately 20 8- to 9-ounce servings.

Easy Vegetable Soup

1	pound ground turkey (or beef)
1/2	cup water
1	medium onion, chopped
1/2	cup celery, chopped
2	cups cabbage, shredded
2	cups vegetables, chopped (green beans, carrots, rutabaga)
1/4	cup instant barley
2	cups water
1	teaspoon Fine Herbes (an old French herb combination)
1	teaspoon chicken bouillon powder
	Spice Island Herb Pepper to taste

Brown meat over medium heat in a 3 quart pot, breaking up meat as it browns. Add 1/2 cup water and simmer for 5 minutes. Drain meat juices into a glass container, skim all fat and return defatted broth to pot. Add remaining ingredients and bring to a boil, adding just enough water to cover vegetables. Simmer about 20 minutes, or until the vegetables are just tender.

Makes 8 one-cup servings.

Potato-Carrot Soup

	"no-stick" cooking spray
6	ounces onion, coarsely chopped
1 3/4	pounds carrots
3/4	pound sweet potato
1/2	pound baking potato
5	cups rich chicken stock (use instant soup base chicken stock)
1	teaspoon salt
1/2	teaspoon freshly ground white pepper
1	tablespoon fresh lemon juice
2	generous tablespoons finely chopped fresh dill
	non-fat sour cream

Preheat the oven to 400°.

Spray medium skillet with no-stick cooking spray, and sauté onion until light golden and just beginning to brown. Scrub carrots and cut into rings, unpeeled. Steam until soft.

Meanwhile, place sweet and white potatoes in oven and bake about 1 hour or until soft.

Scrape sautéed onion into a food processor, deglaze pan with a little of the chicken stock, and add this to the onion. Add carrots and puree. Scoop out potato pulp and add to processor along with salt, white pepper and lemon juice. Puree until thoroughly mixed and very fine. Pour mixture into a saucepan, then add dill and stock. Simmer over very low heat for about 15 minutes.

Soup may be thinned with additional stock. Correct seasoning, and serve warm with a dollop of non-fat sour cream on top.

Serves 6 to 8.

Minestrone Soup

2	tablespoons olive oil
2	cups onion, chopped
2	cups carrots, finely chopped
1	cup cabbage, shredded
7	cups beef broth
5	cups chicken broth
1	medium potato, peeled and diced
1/2	cup orzo
1	medium zucchini, finely chopped
1/2	package frozen chopped spinach
1/2	cup Parmesan cheese
3	tablespoons prepared pesto

In a heavy pan, sauté onion with olive oil over medium heat for 5 minutes. Add carrots and celery. Sauté for 5 minutes. Add the cabbage. Sauté for 5 minutes. Transfer mixture to a large soup pot. Add broth and potatoes to the soup pot. Bring to a boil, lower heat and simmer for 5 minutes. Add spinach, zucchini and orzo. Simmer about 8 to 10 minutes or until orzo and veggies are tender. Add Parmesan cheese and pesto. Mix well. Adjust seasonings and serve. If the soup is too thick for your taste, add more chicken or beef broth to taste.

Makes 6 to 8 servings.

Italian Soup

1	pound turkey sausage
1/2	cup water
1	cup onion, chopped
2	medium cloves garlic, minced
5	cups beef broth
1/2	cup water
1/2	cup red wine
1	cup carrots, sliced thin
1/2	teaspoon basil
1/2	teaspoon oregano
8	ounces tomato sauce
1 1/2	medium zucchini, sliced thin
2	cups tortellini, dry
3	tablespoons fresh parsley
1	green pepper, chopped

Brown sausage in a 4-quart pot until the pink color is gone. Add water, simmer for 5 minutes, and drain liquid into glass container. Skim fat from liquid and return the defatted broth to the pan. Add onion and garlic to meat and sauté for 5 minutes. Add next 6 ingredients and simmer 30 minutes. Add remaining ingredients and simmer an additional 30 minutes. Add additional water if necessary. Serve with grated Parmesan cheese.

Makes 12 one-cup servings.

Chawan-Mushi (Steamed Custard) Japanese Soup

1	chicken breast, boned
6	medium shrimp (optional)
6	eggs
3	cups dashi or light chicken broth
2	tablespoons sake
1/3	cup shoyu (soy sauce)
3	medium-large mushroom caps
1/4	cup cooked peas or 18 canned ginkgo nuts
3	green onions, sliced thin
3	water chestnuts, sliced thin, or 6 thin slices of bamboo shoot
6	spinach leaves or 6 small water cress sprigs

It is preferable to steam raw shelled and deveined shrimp and boned chicken over boiling water or dashi for 5 minutes, or use cooked chicken breast and shrimp. They should be firm enough to slice but still juicy.

Beat eggs slightly and add cooled dashi, sake and shoyu. Mix well. Slice chicken and/or shrimp as thin as possible or dice. Slice mushrooms (if raw ones are used they must be paper thin), and divide these ingredients evenly among 6 one cup bowls or custard cups. Add the other ingredients (any or all), cutting the greens into shreds and dividing everything as evenly as possible. Strain the egg mixture over all and steam over simmering water for 10 to 15 minutes or until custard is set. Overcooking will ruin the dish.

Serves 6.

Golden Broccoli Mushroom Chowder

2	cans or 4 cups chicken stock
2	10 3/4 ounce cans Campbell's broccoli cheese soup
3	medium potatoes, scrubbed and cut into medium chunks
1	bunch broccoli, cut off tips only, avoid use of the stems
1/2	pound fresh mushrooms, cut into large pieces
1	14 1/2 ounce can cream-style corn
3	medium carrots, scrubbed, cut into medium thick cross-sectional slices
1/2	stick butter
1 1/2	cups chopped onion
1	cup chopped fresh parsley
1	pound Velveeta cut into large chunks
1	teaspoon freshly ground pepper

This is a natural for a crock pot. Combine the chicken stock and Campbell's broccoli cheese soup in a large 4-quart crockpot or stockpot. Stir until blended thoroughly. Add the onions, carrots and potatoes and bring to a near boil. Cover and cook for 10 minutes. Add broccoli, parsley, mushrooms, cream-style corn, butter, salt and pepper. Cover and cook for 10 minutes at medium-high heat. Stir in Velveeta. Reduce heat to warm, cover and let simmer or 1 to 2 hours or until carrots are cooked but still firm

Makes approximately 15 cups.

Note: Simmering time can be reduced if the carrots and potatoes are precooked in a microwave in water to cover for about 10 to 12 minutes or until three-quarters of the way cooked. Water can then be drained off.

Schnitz Soup (Fruit Soup)

1	package dried fruit, like apricots, pears, prunes, etc.
1	cup raisins
2	quarts water
1/2	cup sugar
1/2	cup flour
1	cup heavy cream

Cook the fruit in water until well done. Add the sugar and the flour, which has been mixed with the cream until smooth. Bring to a boil. Serve hot.

Gazpacho

2	kilos (or about 4 1/2 pounds) tomatoes
3	cloves garlic
1/2	cup vinegar
1/2	small onion
2	green peppers
2	small cucumbers
1	cup salad oil

Cut the tomatoes, onion, peppers and cucumber in reasonably sized pieces. Put everything in a blender, and working in batches, mix very thoroughly. Serve very cold topped with chopped onion, cucumber, green pepper and tomato.

Makes 6 to 12 servings depending on serving size.

Note: This is true Spanish gazpacho given to me by a neighbor in Madrid.
— Donna Niehous

Turkey Vegetable Soup

Low Salt, Low Fat, Low Cholesterol

1	28-ounce can crushed tomatoes, no salt
1	14 1/2-ounce can stewed tomatoes, no salt
1	16-ounce package frozen mixed vegetables
1	medium onion, diced
1	medium green pepper, diced
1	pound ground turkey
3/4	cup elbow noodles
1	cup lentils
1/2	cup barley
4	28-ounce cans water
1	tablespoon garlic
1	tablespoon black pepper
1	tablespoon basil

In skillet, brown the ground turkey. In a large kettle, add all the ingredients except the elbow noodles. Bring to a boil. Add elbow noodles. Simmer 1 1/2 to 2 hours.

Makes 24 one-cup servings.

Quick Minestrone Soup

3	15-ounce cans chunky style tomatoes with Italian seasoning
4 to 5	cups water
1	medium zucchini, sliced
2	carrots, julienned
1	small onion
8	ounce package frozen broccoli, chopped
8	ounces frozen Italian-style green beans
	pasta shells
	basil
	oregano
	salt

Put the tomatoes, onion, water in a pot, and bring the mixture to a boil. Add the fresh vegetables. Cook 15 to 20 minutes. Add frozen vegetables, and cook until vegetables are tender. Add seasonings to taste. Simmer and remove onions. Add uncooked pasta. Cook until soft. Serve.

Makes 4 to 6 servings.

Mushroom-Barley Soup

2	tablespoons butter or margarine
2	tablespoons olive oil
2	large onions, chopped
1	pound mushrooms, sliced
1	clove garlic, minced
3	tablespoons sweet vermouth or sherry
	salt
	pepper
1	teaspoon paprika
2	bay leaves
3	tablespoons flour
6	cups chicken broth
2/3	cup barley, medium
1	cup (1/2 pint) sour cream

Melt the butter or margarine, add olive oil. Sauté the onions, mushrooms and garlic. Add vermouth or sherry and cook over low heat for 3 to 5 minutes. Blend in spices and flour. Cook over low heat for about 2 minutes. Turn heat to high and add broth gradually, stirring constantly. Bring to a boil. Add barley and turn heat to low. Simmer covered for 30 to 40 minutes. Freeze at this point, if desired. Add sour cream and heat on low, right before serving.

Makes 8 servings.

Taco Beef Soup

1/2	pound ground beef
1/4	cup chopped onion
1 1/2	cups water
1	can 16-ounce stewed tomatoes, cut up
1	can 16-ounce kidney beans
1	can 8-ounce tomato sauce
1/2	envelope, 2 tablespoons, taco seasoning mix
1	small avocado, peeled, seeded and chopped

In a large saucepan cook beef and onion until browned. Drain off excess fat and add water, tomatoes, beans, tomato sauce and taco seasoning. Simmer covered for 15 minutes. Add avocado. Pour into individual bowls and serve with cheese, corn chips and sour cream.

Cold Tomato Cucumber Soup

1	can tomato soup
1	can bouillon
1/2	pint sour cream
2	teaspoons minced onion
1/2	cucumber, peeled, seeded, finely chopped
1/4	teaspoon basil, optional
1/2	teaspoon salt
1	tablespoon red wine

Put all ingredients in a blender for 2 minutes.

Makes 4 servings.

Tennessee Parsnip Soup

4	parsnips, peeled and diced
2	leeks, cut into 1/4 inch slices
2 1/2	cups chicken stock (instant soup base)
1	cup low-fat buttermilk
3	tablespoons white wine
	allspice
1/2	cup chopped watercress leaves
	croutons
	low-fat sour cream

Cook parsnips and leeks in a covered pot about 20 minutes or until tender. Then puree in a food processor or put through a fine sieve.

Combine the puree with the chicken stock.

Add the buttermilk, white wine, a pinch of allspice, and salt and pepper to taste.

Heat the soup just to boiling and stir in chopped watercress leaves.

Garnish with croutons and place a tablespoon of low-fat sour cream on each serving.

Salads

Nick Stellino is the host of <u>Cucina Amore</u>.

Nick Stellino of <u>Cucina Amore's</u> Sweet Pepper Salad

Zio Giovanni used to say, "Non tutti i mali vengono per nuocere." This translates literally to, "Not all bad luck turns out to be bad."

This recipe is a great example of that idea. It is a simple and easy variation upon a delicious but complex classic, "Peperonata," which I developed by mistake while trying to feed myself one frantically busy night while cooking at a restaurant.

4	tablespoons olive oil
1	yellow onion, peeled and quarterd
2	red bell peppers, seeded and cut into 1-inch squares
2	yellow bell peppers, seeded and cut into 1-inch squares
4	garlic cloves, chopped
2	tablespoons chopped, fresh basil
2	tablespoons balsamic vinegar
4-5	ounces mixed baby salad greens (mesclun)
1/4	teaspoon salt
1/8	teaspoon pepper
3	tablespoons crumbled feta cheese

Pour half of the olive oil into a medium non-stick skillet on high heat and cook until it almost reaches the smoking point. While the oil is heating, cut the onion quarters in half crosswise, creating triangles. Cut off the ends and separate the layers with your hands.

When the oil is ready, add the onions and bell peppers and cook on high heat for 2 minutes. Flip the pieces over and cook for 2 more minutes. Add the garlic and basil and cook, stirring for one minute. Add 1 tablespoon of the vinegar, stir and cook for 30 seconds, remove from heat and transfer to a bowl.

In a large salad bowl, mix the greens with the remaining olive oil, remaining vinegar, salt pepper and feta cheese. Toss until everything is well coated. Divide the salad among the serving plates and top with the warm pepper-onion mixture.

Serves 4.

Chicken Salad Berniece

6	chicken breasts
2	tablespoons chives
1/2	teaspoon salt
1/2	teaspoon pepper
2	tablespoons parsley
2	cups celery, chopped
1	cup sour cream
1	tablespoon lemon juice
1	cup mayonnaise
1	tablespoon dry Italian salad dressing

Cook the chicken breasts until tender. Bone and skin the chicken breasts and chop into chunks. Combine chicken, chopped celery, chives, salt, pepper and parsley. Combine sour cream, lemon juice, mayonnaise and dry dressing. Add to chicken mixture and chill.

Makes 10 to 12 servings.

Cobb Salad

1	large head romaine lettuce, washed
2	avocados, peeled and chopped
3	tomatoes, cut in small dice
1	cup bleu cheese, crumbled
4	green onions, chopped or 1 small red onion, chopped
4	ounces cooked chicken breast, cut in small pieces
2	hard-boiled eggs, chopped

Green Goddess Dressing

1/2	can anchovies
4	tablespoons chopped parsley
2	tablespoons chopped basil or tarragon
2	tablespoons chopped chives
	small bunch watercress, leaves only
1 1/2	cups mayonnaise
1	tablespoon white wine vinegar

Dry the lettuce and cut it into strips. Tear the strips into small pieces and put them into a salad bowl. Arrange all of the ingredients on top.

To make the dressing, combine all the ingredients in a blender or food processor and puree until smooth and very green. Serve the dressing separately with the salad.

Taboule Salad (Cracked Wheat Salad)

1	clove garlic, diced
1/2	teaspoon salt
1	fresh lemon, juice and pulp
2/3	cup bulgar wheat
1	bunch green scallions, finely chopped, including 2 inches of green tips
1 2/3	cups fresh parsley, chopped
1/4	cup mint, finely chopped or 1 tablespoon dried mint
1/4	cup olive oil, (preferably extra-virgin)
1/2	teaspoon fresh black pepper
1	pint ripe cherry tomatoes, diced, reserve 6 for decoration
2	cucumbers, pared, seeded and diced
	romaine lettuce leaves

Place garlic, salt and fresh lemon juice in a large bowl and pound or mash together. In a small bowl, soak the bulgar wheat in cool water to cover for about 20 minutes. Drain and squeeze out extra moisture. Add the moist bulgar to the lemon mixture. Add scallions, parsley and mint. Toss lightly, sprinkling with oil and pepper. Mix thoroughly, taste and correct seasoning to your liking. Add cherry tomatoes and cucumbers. Toss lightly. Cover and chill well. To serve, arrange romaine lettuce leaves around a serving platter with the stems to the center. Mound the salad in the center and onto each leaf. Decorate with remaining cherry tomato halves. Use the romaine to scoop the salad to serve.

Makes 6 servings.

Summer Rice Salad

2	cups rice
4	cups chicken salad
1	inch piece of fresh ginger
1	teaspoon curry powder
1/2	teaspoon tumeric
1/4	cup olive oil
	juice of 2 small lemons
1/2	cup white raisins
1/2	cup raisins or currants
1	cup green pepper, chopped
1	cup mayonnaise
1/2	cup sour cream
1/2	cup sliced almonds
1/4	cup chopped parsley

Cook rice in stock with ginger and tumeric. Toss cooked rice with olive oil and lemon juice, salt and pepper. Let stand overnight. Toss with raisins, green pepper and enough mayonnaise and sour cream to bind. Sprinkle almonds and parsley on top.

Makes 8 servings.

Cauliflower Salad

1	small head lettuce, cut into chunks
1	small head cauliflower, separated into bite-sized pieces, raw
1 1/4	cups frozen peas
1	cup Hellmann's mayonnaise
1	envelope Good Season's Mild Italian dry dressing
	generous sprinkling of Parmesan cheese, grated

Combine lettuce and cauliflower in large bowl. Top with remaining ingredients. Let sit, covered tightly, in refrigerator at least 1/2 day or overnight. Toss well just before serving.

Serves 8 to 10 people.

Bacon and Broccoli Salad

1/4-1/2	head broccoli, cut into small pieces
4	slices bacon, fried crisp and crumbled
1/4	cup raisins
2	tablespoons chopped onion
1/2	cup mayonnaise
1	tablespoon vinegar
2	tablespoons sugar
1/2	cup shredded cheddar cheese

Combine the first four ingredients. Combine the mayonnaise, vinegar and sugar. Toss with vegetables. Stir in cheese and refrigerate. For reduced calorie and fat content, use Miracle Light dressing, imitation bacon bits, light cheese and sweetener.

Makes 4 servings.

Mom's Good-for-Christmas-or-Anytime Molded Salad

2	3-ounce packages lime gelatin
1	8-ounce package cream cheese, cut into small cubes
1/2	cup chopped walnuts
1/2	cup chopped celery
1	pint coffee cream or half & half
2	cups canned, crushed pineapple, drained but reserve juice (crushed pineapple in heavy syrup may be used rather than in its own juice if very sweet taste is desired)
2	cups hot pineapple juice (hot water may be added to make up to 2 cups liquid if not enough juice from canned pineapple)

Bring pineapple juice to just below a boil, but do not boil. Stir gelatin into pineapple juice.

Add cream cheese in bits. Add celery and chopped nuts. Add crushed pineapple. After this mixture is cooled, add pint of coffee cream or half & half. Mix well and pour into decorative mold or 9 by 13 inch glass casserole. Chill. Serve on a bed of lettuce. May use fruit dressing on top.

Pineapple-Carrot Molded Salad

1 1/2	small (3-ounce) packages lemon-flavored gelatin
2/3	cup hot water
1	20-ounce can crushed pineapple, drained
2/3	cup pineapple juice
2/3	cup canned evaporated milk
2	tablespoons vinegar
1	8-ounce package creamed cheese
1	cup carrots, cut into 1 inch pieces

Put gelatin and very hot water in blender and pour in pineapple juice and vinegar. Blend. Add milk, blending continuously. Blend in cream cheese. After this is well blended, add crushed pineapple and carrots.

Chill in decorative mold or 9 by 13 inch casserole dish. Serve on bed of lettuce.

Christopher D. Glass's Asparagus Salad with Shrimp, Herbs and Marinated Tomatoes

Christopher D. Glass is from Jacques at the Findlay Inn and Conference Center.

3	ounces green asparagus
3	ounces white asparagus
2 1/2	ounces shrimpettes
6-8	leaves Belgian endive
1/2	teaspoon each fresh chervil, basil, tarragon, and finely chopped chilies
1/2	cup finely chopped shallots
1/2	teaspoon fresh lemon juice
1 1/2	teaspoons champagne vinegar
1 1/2	teaspoons white wine
2	tablespoons olive oil
	salt and pepper to taste

Marinated Tomatoes

2	Roma tomatoes
2	teaspoons finely diced red onion
1	tablespoon raspberry vinegar
1/2	teaspoon fresh cracked black pepper
	salt to taste

Peel white and green asparagus, blanche in boiling salted water briefly. Then cool immediately in ice water. Remove and reserve. Chop herbs finely and reserve. Mix vinegar, shallots, white wine, olive oil, salt and pepper. Combine shrimp with lemon juice, arrange asparagus and shrimp mixture with endive on a plate drizzle with dressing.

For Marinated Tomatoes: Core and score bottoms of tomatoes, blanche in boiling water 7 to 10 seconds. Remove and cool in ice water. Peel skins off tomatoes. Cut in half, rinse and remove seeds. Dice tomatoes into 1/8 inch cubes and finely dice the red onion. Add vinegar, black pepper and salt to taste. Arrange tomatoes in neat piles around asparagus salad.

Kelly's Potato Salad

5	pounds boiled red potatoes, cubed with skins on
3	eggs, boiled and cubed
1/2	small onion, chopped
1	greeen pepper, chopped
1/2	cup Tony Packo's Pickles and Peppers, chopped
1/2	cup celery, chopped
1	pint sour cream
1	cup mayonnaise
2	tablespoons vinegar
1/4	cup sugar
	salt and pepper to taste
	dill weed and fresh parsley to garnish

Boil eggs and potatoes separately until cooked. Cool and cut into cubes. Add onion, green pepper, celery and pickles. Mix in sour cream, mayonnaise, vinegar and sugar, salt and pepper. Garnish with fresh parsley and sprinkle of dill weed.

Makes 6 to 8 servings.

Cajun Potato Salad

5	pounds cooked potatoes
2/3	cup each, celery, onion and green pepper, diced
12	hard boiled eggs, chopped
3	tablespoons Cajun or Dijon mustard
1	tablespoon crushed garlic
1	tablespoon red wine vinegar
1	tablespoon sugar
1	teaspoon salt
1-1 1/2	cups Cajun mayonnaise

Mayonnaise

1	egg
1	yolk
1/2	teaspoon cayenne pepper
1	tablespoon lemon juice
2	teaspoon Worcestershire sauce
1 1/4	cups olive oil

For mayonnaise: Place eggs in a tall glass and top with oil. Using a stab blender, raise it gradually until all of oil is mixed. Stir in remaining ingredients.

For salad: Place all other ingredients in a bowl and mix gently with mayonnaise.

Taco Salad

1	pound ground beef
1	1 1/4 ounce package taco seasoning
1	medium head lettuce
1	small can kidney beans, drained
1	large onion, chopped
8	ounces cheddar cheese, grated
1	package Doritos, crushed

Dressing
(best if made the day before)

8	ounces Thousand Island dressing
1	tablespoon taco seasoning
1/3	cup sugar
1	tablespoon taco sauce

Brown ground beef and add taco seasoning, saving 1 tablespoon for dressing. Layer the salad ingredients starting with the lettuce and ending with the cheese. Add the dressing and chips just before serving.

Makes 10 to 12 servings.

Hungarian Sausage Salad

4	small potatoes
1/2	cup oil
3	tablespoons wine vinegar
1	teaspoon Dijon mustard
1	teaspoon dill seeds, slightly crushed
1	tablespoon chopped parsley
1	teaspoon chopped dill
	a pinch of hot paprika
	salt
1	pound sausage such as kielbasa, smoked pork sausage, knockwurst or bratwurst
1	large red onion, thinly sliced
2	green peppers, cored and sliced
4	tomatoes, quartered

Scrub and peel the potatoes and cook in salted water in a covered saucepan for 20 minutes or until soft.

Mix all the dressing ingredients in a medium-sized bowl. Dice the potatoes while still warm and coat with dressing. Leave the potatoes to cool in the dressing. If using knockwurst boil for 5 minutes. Broil the bratwurst until browned on all sides. Slice the sausage in half inch slices and combine with the onion, pepper and tomatoes. Carefully combine with the potatoes in the dressing, taking care not to overmix and break up the potatoes. Pile into a large serving dish and allow to stand for one hour before serving.

Salmon Pasta Salad with Peas

3	cups uncooked shell macaroni
2	6 1/2-ounce cans salmon, drained and flaked
1	6-ounce jar marinated artichoke hearts, chilled and drained
1/4	cup Italian dressing
2	tablespoons capers, drained (optional)
1	package frozen peas
1/4	cup Parmesan cheese

Cook the macaroni according to directions on the package. Drain and rinse with cold water. Cook peas according to package. Mix macaroni and other remaining ingredients. Add salmon before serving.

Makes 4 servings.

Italian Pasta Salad

1	pound pasta shapes
8	ounces assorted Italian meats such as salami, prosciutto, coppa, breasola, cut in strips
4	ounces provolone cheese, cut in strips
15	black olives, halved
4	tablespoons small capers
4	ounces peas
1	small red onion or 2 shallots, chopped
6	ounces mushrooms, stems trimmed and sliced

Dressing

3	tablespoons white wine vinegar
1/2	cup olive oil
1/2	clove garlic, minced
1	teaspoon fennel seed, crushed
1	tablespoon chopped parsley
1	tablespoon chopped basil
1	tablespoon mustard
	salt and pepper

Cook the pasta in a large saucepan of boiling water with a pinch of salt just until tender. Add the frozen peas during the last 3 minutes of cooking time. Drain the pasta and peas and rinse under hot water. Leave in cold water until ready to use. Mix the dressing ingredients together well and drain the pasta and peas thoroughly. Mix the pasta and peas with the Italian meats and cheese, olives, capers, chopped onion or shallot and sliced mushrooms. Pour the dressing over the salad and toss all the ingredients together to coat. Do not overmix.

Chill for up to 1 hour before serving.

Salmon Salad with Cucumber Dressing

1	cup minced cucumbers
1/2	teaspoon salt
1	tablespoon fresh dill weed
1	cup sour cream
1	head romaine lettuce, torn
1 1/2	cups salmon chunks, freshly cooked or canned
1 1/2	cups thinly sliced celery
1 1/2	cups broccoli cuts, crisply cooked
1 1/2	cups cherry tomatoes

Thoroughly drain cucumbers for 2 to 3 hours.

Mix salt, dill weed and sour cream. Add cucumbers and chill.

Place the remaining ingredients in a large bowl. Pour dressing over and toss lightly.

Lumpzy's Salad

Salad

6	red potatoes
2	medium Idaho potatoes
1	onion, in chunks
1	small stalk broccoli
8 to 10	radishes, sliced
1	cucumber, sliced
1	cup golden raisins
1	teaspoon celery seed
1	tablespoon dry parsley
4	hard boiled eggs

Dressing

1/4	cup Marzetti fat-free slaw dressing
1	tablespoon prepared mustard
4	tablespoons balsamic vinegar
1/2	teaspoon salt
1/2	teaspoon pepper
1	teaspoon sugar

Peel Idaho potatoes, but leave the skins on the red potatoes. Cut the potatoes into chunks. Put the potatoes and onions in water in a 3-quart casserole. Zap in a microwave until tender. Cut broccoli into small pieces. Add radishes, raisins, celery seed, cucumbers, parsley and sliced eggs to the hot potatoes. Add dressing. Toss. Eat warm or refrigerate for 1 hour before serving.

Makes 6 to 8 servings.

Three-Bean Salad

1	14 1/2-ounce can green beans
1	14 1/2-ounce can yellow beans
1	14 1/2-ounce can red kidney beans
1/2	cup green pepper, chopped finely
1/2	cup onion, chopped or in rings
3/4	cup sugar
1/4	cup salad oil
1/3	cup vinegar
	salt and pepper to taste

Pour liquid from beans. In a large bowl, mix beans, green peppers and onions. Mix the remaining ingredients. Pour over the bean mixture and refrigerate for several hours. Serve cold. Can be made a day ahead of time.

Makes 8 to 10 servings.

Mariner's Salad

1	pound pasta shells, plain or spinach
4	large scallops, cleaned
1	cup frozen mussels, defrosted
1/2	cup lemon juice and water mixed
4	ounces shelled and de-veined shrimp
1/2	cup cockles or small clams, cooked
4	crab sticks, cut in small pieces
4	green onions, chopped
1	tablespoon chopped parsley

Dressing

	grated rind and juice of 1/2 lemon
1	cup mayonnaise
2	teaspoons paprika
1/3	cup sour cream or plain yogurt
	salt and pepper

Cook the pasta for 10 minutes in a large pan of boiling salted water with 1 tablespoon of oil. Drain and rinse under hot water. Leave in cold water until ready to use. Cook the scallops and mussels in the lemon juice and water mixture for about 5 minutes or until fairly firm. Cut the scallops into 2 or 3 pieces, depending upon size.

Mix the dressing and drain the pasta thoroughly. Mix together to coat completely with dressing. Stir carefully so that the shellfish do not break up. Chill for up to 1 hour before serving.

Layered Chicken Salad

Salad

1	package pea pods
6	cups lettuce
1	cucumber
1/4	pound bean sprouts
1	cup water chestnuts
1/2	cup green onions
4	cups chicken breast

Sauce

2	cups mayonnaise
2	teaspoons curry
1/2	tablespoon ginger
1	tablespoon sugar

Blanche the pea pods. Slice the cucumbers thinly as well as the water chestnuts. Cube the chicken breast.

Layer salad ingredients in serving dish. Spread sauce across the top.

Combine the mayonnaise, curry, ginger and sugar. Serve the salad accompanied with peanuts, cherry tomatoes and chutney in small bowls.

Popoli and Potato Salad

2	pounds octopus cooked and cleaned, cut into bite-sized pieces
2	pounds waxy potatoes, cooked in skins, peeled and sliced
1	medium red onion, diced
1	red bell pepper, thinly sliced
1/4	cup parsley, preferably Italian, chopped
1/4	cup fresh basil, chopped

Lemon Vinaigrette

1/3	cup fresh lemon juice
2	tablespoons red wine vinegar
2	teaspoons sugar
1	teaspoon salt
1	tablespoon Dijon mustard
2/3	cup olive oil

For popoli and potato salad: To cook the octopus, simply put it in a pot of simmering water. Cover and cook for 2 hours. Then remove from pot, cool, pull the skin off and cut it up.

For vinaigrette: Place all ingredients in a bowl and pour enough vinaigrette to coat. Toss gently and allow to set a bit to blend flavors.

Green Beans En Salada

1	pound fresh green beans
3	cloves fresh garlic
	fresh parsley
	olive oil
	garlic salt, salt and pepper

Snap off the ends of the beans and wash thoroughly. Drop in a pot of boiling salted water. Cook until the beans are tender. Drain and cool to room temperature. Add fresh cut parsley, slices of garlic, salt, pepper, garlic salt and oil to taste. Toss and refrigerate. The salad is more flavorful if eaten the day after it is prepared.

Makes 4 to 6 servings.

Chicken Salad

1	cup mayonnaise
3/4	cup sour cream
1 1/2	tablespoons lemon juice
1 1/2	teaspoons salt
5	cups diced, cooked chicken
2	cups celery, diced
1	cup cashew halves
1	cup seedless white grapes

Toss lightly. Serve on lettuce leaves. Refrigerate. The salad can be made one day ahead.

Makes 8 servings.

Oriental Cabbage Salad

Salad

2	packages Oriental ramen noodles, chicken or mushroom flavor
1	large head or 8 to 10 cups cabbage, shredded
1/4	cup sliced green onion
4	tablespoons sesame seeds

Dressing

6	tablespoons vinegar
4	tablespoons sugar
4	tablespoons sesame or salad oil
1/2-1	teaspoon white pepper
1/2	teaspoon salt
	seasoning packets from noodles
1	cup slivered almonds (optional)

In a large bowl, mix the crushed noodles, cabbage, green onions and sesame seeds.

Mix the dressing ingredients in a small bowl and pour over salad. Toss to coat well. Sprinkle the slivered almonds over the salad if desired and serve

Makes 8 to 10 servings.

Winter Salad Lunch

	raw carrot, sliced
	stick of celery
1/4	yellow pepper
	wedge of iceberg lettuce
1/3	can partially drained Del Monte original stewed tomatoes
	small helping large curd cottage cheese
	generous dab Hellmann's mayonnaise

Cut the celery, pepper and lettuce into bite-size pieces. Mix all the ingredients and serve cold. Multiply the ingredients by the number of people you wish to serve. Hint: Corn muffins go well with this lunch.

Korean Salad

Salad

1	large bag spinach, washed, dried and then torn into bite-sized pieces
1	large can bean sprouts, well drained
8	bacon strips, cooked crisp, drained and crumbled
3	hard boiled eggs, diced
1	small can water chestnuts, drained and sliced

Dressing

1	medium onion, chopped
1	cup vegetable oil
1/4	cup vinegar
3/4	cup sugar, or less to taste
1/3	cup catsup
1	tablespoon Worcestershire sauce
1/4	teaspoon salt.

Assemble the salad in a large bowl and chill. Combine the dressing ingredients and chill. Just before serving, pour the dressing over salad and toss gently but thoroughly.

Serves 8 to 10 amply.

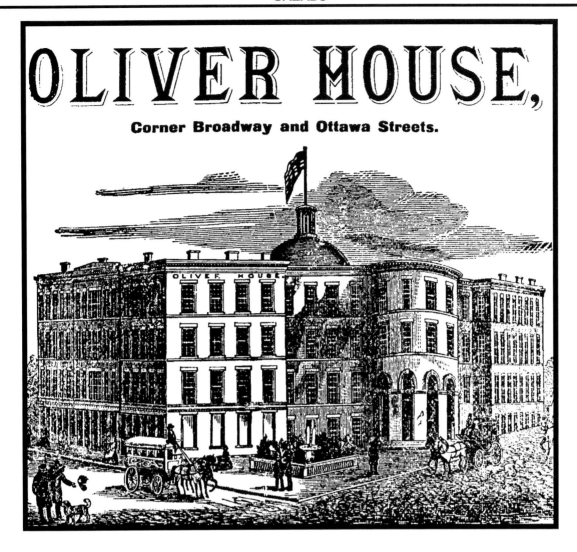

OLIVER HOUSE,
Corner Broadway and Ottawa Streets.

Oliver House Chicken Salad

This updated Chicken Salad was served at the Grand Opening of the Oliver House in 1859. It was originally listed on the Bill of Fare as Chicken en Mayonnaise.

10	pounds fresh chicken breasts
2	small cans sliced water chestnuts
1	pound toasted slivered almonds
1	bunch green onions, sliced 1/4-inch thick
1	large red pepper, cut into thin strips
1	tablespoon ground ginger
1 1/2	tablespoons Lawry's seasoned salt
1/2	cup sugar
3/4	gallon Hellmann's mayonnaise
12	ounces fresh squeezed lemon juice
1/4	cup Dijon mustard

Lay out chicken breast on sheet pan and cover with aluminum foil. (For better results, season with Lawry's seasoned salt and drizzle with lemon.) Bake at 300° until done. Cool, then dice into small pieces. In large mixing bowl combine sugar, ginger, seasoned salt, mayonnaise, lemon juice and dijon mustard. Mix well and add remaining ingredients. Toss, chill and serve.

Yield: 20 pounds

Mikan Salad (mee-kahn)

A Cross Culture Salad of Beef, Endive, Orange and Sesame (Japanese-American-French)

1	tablespoon salad oil
8	ounces thinly sliced beef tips
2	ounces ginger root, peeled and cut into 1/8 by 1/2 inch strips
4	ounces daikon, peeled and cut into 1/8 by 1/2 inch strips
4	ounces Spanish onion, peeled and cut into 1/4 inch dice
8	ounces washed bok choy cabbage, stemmed and cut into 1/4 inch dice, reserve the dark leaves for salad
	salt, white pepper, black pepper mix
1	head endives, washed, and cut into 3/4 inch cubes
2	oranges, grate zest of orange and reserve
2	oranges, peeled, sliced 1/8 inch thin, cut into halfmoons
1	teaspoon sesame oil
1	tablespoon toasted sesame seeds
2	ounces teriyaki sauce

Teriyaki Sauce

4	ounces beef scraps
2	ounces onions
1	ounce carrots
1	ounce celery
1/2	head garlic
2	ounces sliced ginger
1	cup beef broth
1/2	cup Mirin wine
1	cup Kikkoman soy sauce
1	cup lite corn syrup
	corn starch

To prepare teriyaki sauce, fry the beef in a 2 quart sauce pan. Add onions, carrots and celery to beef and brown. Add garlic and ginger to mixture and fry. Add beef broth. Add wine and deglaze pan with a wooden spoon. Add soy sauce and corn syrup and bring to a boil.

Reduce heat to a simmer. Simmer for 1 hour, then strain at boil. Adjust seasoning with sugar or soy sauce and thicken with a wash of cornstarch and Mirin wine until it coats the back of the spoon.

To prepare salad, heat oil in sturdy wok or sauté pan, add beef, sauté quickly to brown, remove and reserve. Reheat oil and add ginger, onions, daikon and bok choy stems. Season with salt and pepper mix. Fry 1 minute until very hot and add beef back to vegetables. Remove from heat and season with orange zest, sesame oil, sesame seeds and teriyaki sauce. Arrange lettuces and orange slices on plate or platter. Top with warm beef and vegetables, dribble with juices and garnish with orange zest and sesame seeds. Serve immediately with steamed rice and miso soup.

Serves 4

Caesar Salad Dressing

1	teaspoon Worcestershire sauce
1/4	teaspoon salt
1/4	teaspoon dry mustard
1	large clove garlic, crushed
1	egg
1	tablespoon lemon juice
3/4	cup freshly grated Parmesan cheese
3/4	cup olive oil

Combine first 6 ingredients in a food processor. Add olive oil in a steady stream. Add Parmesan cheese and just combine. Adjust seasonings.

Refrigerate. Use as a dressing over torn romaine lettuce or as a dip for veggies.

Makes 1 1/2 cups.

Tangy Low-Fat Ranch Dressing

1	cup nonfat sour cream
1	cup reduced fat mayonnaise
2	tablespoons chopped fresh dill weed (or 2 teaspoon dried)
1	tablespoon fresh lemon juice
1	teaspoon salt
1/2	teaspoon crushed garlic
1/4	teaspoon fresh ground pepper

Mix all ingredients and chill.

Makes 2 cups.

Broccoli Salad

4	stalks fresh chopped broccoli
1/2	cup chopped onions
1/2	cup raisins
1/4	cup sugar
10	strips crisp-fried bacon, crumbled
3	tablespoons slivered almonds
1	cup mayonnaise
3	tablespoons vinegar

Mix broccoli, onions and raisins. Add mayonnaise, vinegar and sugar. After tossing wih crumbled bacon and slivered almonds, chill.

Seafood Main Dishes

Mary Ann Esposito's Scampi con Linguine e Limone (Shrimp with Linguine and Lemon)

Recipe from Nella Cucina, by Mary Ann Esposito, host of <u>Ciao Italia</u>.

1	pound large shrimp, in the shell
6	tablespoons extra-virgin olive oil
1	large clove garlic, peeled and cut in half lengthwise
1	small dried hot red pepper, cut in half lengthwise
3/4	pound linguine
1/2	teaspoon fine sea salt, or more to taste
	freshly ground black pepper
3	tablespoons fresh lemon juice
1	tablespoon grated lemon zest
3	tablespoons fresh parsley, finely chopped

In a medium saucepan, bring about 6 cups of water to a boil. Add the shrimp and cook about 2 to 3 minutes or just until the shells turn pink. Drain the shrimp in a colander and cool. Shell and devein the shrimp, then cut in half lengthwise, but not through the tail, set aside.

In a large skillet, heat the olive oil with the garlic and red pepper. Sauté very slowly, pressing on the garlic and pepper with a wooden spoon to extract juice. Remove and discard the garlic when it starts to soften and turn golden. Remove the pepper when soft and discard. Set skillet aside.

In a large pot, bring 4 to 6 quarts of water to a boil. Add the linguine and boil until al dente, or firm but not mushy.

While the linguine is cooking, reheat the skillet, add the shrimp, and sauté for about 2 minutes. Sprinkle in the sea salt and pepper.

Drain the linguine in a colander and immediately add to the shrimp. Add the lemon juice, zest and parsley. Toss well. Transfer to a large platter and serve immediately.

Stephen C. Brownson's Individually Baked Salmon Lasagna with Tomato Basil Butter Sauce

Stephen C. Brownson is the Chef and Owner of Stephen's Restaurant in Perrysburg.

Picture on page 181.

Lasagna

6	oven proof ramekins, 6-8 ounce size
1/2	pound clean, large, flat, spinach leaves blanched
12	pieces pre-cooked lasagna noodles cut to fit ramekins
12	ounces salmon filets, skinned and boned
5	tablespoons olive oil (in all)
4	large tomatoes peeled, seeded and chopped
3	shallots, minced
6	tablespoons chopped fresh basil
1	tablespoon minced garlic
12	ounces goat cheese

Sauce

1	shallot, minced
1/4	cup dry white wine
1/4	cup chicken stock or broth
1-1/2	cups heavy cream
8	tablespoons unsalted butter, cut in small pieces
4	tomatoes, peeled and seeded
8	tablespoons fresh basil, julienne cut

For the Lasagna: With a pastry brush or paper towel, take 2 tablespoons of the olive oil and lightly coat the inside of the ramekins. Line them with spinach leaves, cover and wait to assemble. Heat a sauté pan. Add the remaining olive oil. Sauté the garlic, shallot, tomato and fresh basil. Season with salt and fresh ground black pepper. Remove from pan and allow to cool.

To assemble: Place one circle of pasta in each of the ramekins. Next, place one ounce of thinly sliced salmon atop the pasta, then a small layer of the tomato mixture, then one ounce of the goat cheese then another pasta circle and repeat. Fold the spinach leaves over the top and cover with both plastic wrap and aluminum foil. Bake at 350° for 15-20 minutes.

For the Sauce: Combine the shallot, white wine and chicken stock and reduce at medium heat until almost dry. Add the cream and reduce by half. Swirl in the butter a little at a time. Finely dice 2 tomatoes, reserve. Puree the other 2 tomatoes in a food processor and add to the sauce, add fresh basil. Adjust seasoning.

To serve: Pour equal amounts of sauce on warmed plates. Remove cooked lasagna from ramekins. Cut in half and place over sauce. Garnish with finely diced tomatoes and a fresh basil leaf.

Serves 6.

Jacques Pepin's Broiled Red Snapper with Lemon Vinaigrette

From The Short-Cut Cook (Morrow 1990) by Jacques Pepin, Host of <u>Today's Gourmet II.</u>

4	fillets (1 1/4 pounds total) red snapper, with skin
1/2	teaspoon salt
1/4	teaspoon freshly ground pepper
2	teaspoons corn or canola oil

Lemon Vinaigrette

2	tablespoons olive oil
2	teaspoons lemon juice
1/4	teaspoon salt
1/4	teaspoon freshly ground black pepper
1	tablespoon chopped chives

Place the fillets skin side up on a work surface, and cut two diagonal slits about 1/4 inch deep through the skin of each one. This helps the fish absorb the marinade more readily and cook more evenly.

Place the fillets in a plastic bag along with the 1/2 teaspoon salt, 1/4 teaspoon pepper, and the corn oil. Seal the bag and toss to mix the ingredients well. Refrigerate for at least an hour before cooking.

Arrange the fillet skin side up in a single layer on a baking sheet lined with aluminum foil in a gratin dish from which they can be served. Place under a preheated broiler, no more than 4 inches from the heat, and broil for 5 minutes.

Meanwhile, make the vinaigrette: Combine the olive oil, lemon juice, 1/4 teaspoon salt and 1/4 teaspoon pepper in a bowl, and blend well.

Remove the fish from the broiler. The skin should be bubbly, brown and crusty. Spoon the vinaigrette over the fish, sprinkle with chives, and serve immediately.

Makes 4 servings

If snapper is not available, substitute striped bass, black bass or another variety of very fresh fish fillets.

Walleye Wellington

6	walleye or pickerel fillets
18-20	shitake mushrooms
4	young scallions
2	cans Alaskan crabmeat
3/4	cup mayonnaise or Dijon mustard
6	sheets phyllo dough
2	well-beaten egg yolks

Finely chop mushrooms and scallions.

Mix with crabmeat and mayonnaise or mustard. Set aside.

Place fish fillets in center of phyllo sheets. Spoon the mushroom/crabmeat mixture across the top of the fish. Carefully fold the dough over the fish, and place on a lightly oiled baking sheet. If desired, decorate the tops with left over dough. Brush tops with egg yolk. Bake for approximately 8 minutes at 300°. Dough should be crusty and shiny. Serve warm or at room temperature. Garnish serving plate with lemon rosettes placed on lemon balm or fresh mint.

Crab Crepes

Crab Filling and Sauce

1	6-ounce package Wakefield snow crab or king crab meat
1/4	cup butter or margarine
1/3	cup chopped green onions
1	cup thinly sliced celery
1	cup chopped mushrooms
3	tablespoons flour
1 1/3	cups milk
1/3	cup grated Swiss cheese
1/4	teaspoon salt
1/8	teaspoon pepper
	dash nutmeg
8	cooked crepes
	Parmesan cheese, grated (optional)

Crepes

3	eggs
2 1/4	cups milk
1 1/2	cups flour
1	teaspoon salt
1/2	teaspoon baking powder
	butter

For crepes: With rotary beater or mixer, beat 3 eggs well. Add the milk, flour, salt and baking powder, and beat until smooth. Heat a heavy 9 inch skillet or crepe pan and brush it lightly with butter.

Add a third of a cup of batter to the skillet, tilting to coat the bottom. Cook over medium to medium-high heat until golden brown. Remove the crepe to a dish towel. Repeat with the remaining batter, greasing skillet as necessary. Makes 10 to 11 crepes.

Crepes may be wrapped air-tight and refrigerated for 2 to 3 days or frozen for 2 to 3 months.

Thaw crabmeat, retain liquid and separate into chunks. In saucepan, sauté onions, celery and mushrooms in butter or margarine for 2 to 3 minutes. Remove with slotted spoon and set aside. Stir flour into remaining butter or margarine until smooth. Add milk and crab liquid. Cook until thickened. Stir in cheese, salt, pepper and nutmeg. In small bowl, toss together crab, onions, celery, mushrooms and 1/2 cup of sauce. Season to taste. Spread equal amounts of the filling across the center of each crepe and roll up or fold over. Place in shallow baking pan and pour remaining sauce over top. Sprinkle with Parmesan cheese, if desired. Heat in 350° oven for 10 to 15 minutes.

Makes 8 crepes.

Bell Peppers with Seafood Stuffing

6	large green peppers
4	tablespoon butter
1	large onion, chopped coarse
1/2	cup diced celery
1/2	pound large shrimp, cooked, peeled and deveined
1	tablespoon flour
3	tablespoons red pepper sauce
	salt and pepper
2	cups cooked white rice
1	6-ounce can crab meat
	bread crumbs

Cut off the stem tops from the green peppers, and remove the seeds and membranes. Parboil the peppers for 5 minutes and drain. Place in a greased baking dish and stuff.

In a large skillet, sauté the onions and celery in butter for 5 minutes.

Add the shrimp, flour, tomato sauce, the dash of red pepper sauce and salt and pepper to taste. Simmer for 10 minutes.

Add white rice and crab meat to the simmered mixture and stuff peppers. Top with bread crumbs and bake 30 minutes at 350°.

Fifi Berry's Shrimp & Scallop Sauté with Lobster Dill Sauce

Picture on page 129.

8	ounces shrimp 16-20 ct. peeled and deveined
8	ounces sea scallops 10-20 ct. cleaned
1	cup fish stock
2/3	teaspoon shallots minced
2/3	teaspoon garlic minced
1	teaspoon fresh chopped dill
1	ounce whipping cream
4	pieces white bread (for toast points)
	Kosher salt (to taste)

Fish Stock (yield 1/2 gallon)

1	pound lobster shells
8	ounces shrimp shells
5	pounds bones from a white fleshed fish, preferably Halibut
1	quart white wine, Chablis
1	leek chopped, white only
8	ounces mushrooms chopped
2	lemons cut in half

Sear shells in hot oil (vegetable and pomace). Add wine and rest of the ingredients. Add cold water until all ingredients are covered with one inch water. Slowly bring to a boil. Simmer for 30-40 minutes.

Skim off oil and foam during the simmer. Cool. Bring one cup of strained fish stock to a boil with the shallots, garlic and dill. Remove from heat and add cream and salt. Lightly flour shrimp and scallops. Add scallops and cook for 2 minutes. Turn over and continue cooking for 1 minute. Add sauce and simmer for 2 minutes. Serve on toast points.

Serving suggestion: Serve with steamed fresh asparagus spears.

Crab and Shrimp Casserole

1 1/2	pounds crabmeat
1/2	pound small shrimp
1/2	green pepper, chopped
1/3	cup parsley, chopped
2	cups cooked rice
1 1/2	cup real mayonnaise
2	packages frozen green peas, thawed but uncooked
	salt and pepper to taste

Toss all ingredients lightly. Place in greased casserole. Refrigerate, covered. Bake for 1 hour at 350° covered.

Serves 6.

Marsala Fish

4	medium sized mackeral, trout or similar fish
	juice of 1 lemon
2	teaspoon tumeric
2	green chili peppers, finely chopped
1	small piece ginger, grated
1	clove garlic, finely minced
	a pinch ground cinammon
	a pinch ground cloves
4	tablespoons oil
	salt and pepper
	fresh coriander leaves

Accompaniment

1/2	cucumber, finely diced
1/2	cup thick, plain yogurt
1	green onion, finely chopped
	salt and pepper

Clean and gut the fish. Cut three slits on each side of the fish. Combine spices, lemon juice, oil, garlic and chili peppers and spread over the fish and inside the cuts. Place whole sprigs of coriander inside the fish. Brush the grill rack lightly with oil or use a wire fish rack. Cook the fish 10 to 15 minutes, turning often and basting with any remaining mixture. Combine the accompaniment ingredients and serve with the fish.

Russian Fruit and Shrimp Boat

1	pound shrimp, cooked and deveined
3	cups assorted melon balls, drained
1	cup pineapple chunks, drained
1/4	cup Wish Bone Russian dressing

In a large bowl, combine shrimp, melon balls, pineapple chunks and Russian dressing. Cover and refrigerate at least one hour. It may be mounded in a melon basket or pineapple shells in lettuce cups.

Makes 6 to 8 servings.

Phyllo-wrapped Salmon

6	salmon steaks
6	sheets phyllo dough
	melted butter
1	pound washed spinach
1	pound feta cheese
	lemon pepper

Butter the sheets of phyllo and fold in half lengthwise. Sprinkle lemon pepper on the salmon steaks and place the steaks at the bottom of the phyllo sheets. Sprinkle crumbled feta (3 or 4 tablespoons or to taste) on steak, then place 6 to 8 spinach leaves on top of the cheese. Fold steak, spinach, and feta, like the American flag (triangularly) and place on buttered baking pan. Bake for 20 to 30 minutes in preheated 350° oven.

Makes 6 servings.

Gourmet Crab Ring

1	teaspoon unflavored gelatin
1/4	cup cold water
2	8-ounce packages cream cheese, softened
2	tablespoon cooking sherry
3/4	teaspoon seasoned salt
1	2-ounce jar pimentos, sliced, drained and chopped
1	6-ounce package frozen king crabmeat, thawed, drained and cut up
1/8	teaspoon ground black pepper
1/4	cup snipped parsley
	a small amount onion, chopped very fine (optional)

Sprinkle gelatin over water in a double boiler to soften. Stir until dissolved. Beat this mixture into the cream cheese until the cheese is smooth. Stir in next 5 to 6 ingredients and 2 tablespoons of the parsley. Pour into 3 cup ring mold. Refrigerate at least 4 hours, or until set. To serve, turn out on plate. Garnish with the remaining parsley. Place parsley sprigs in center. Serve with crackers.

Makes 3 cups.

George Hirsch and Marie Bianco's Swordfish with Olive Relish

From Gather 'Round the Grill by George Hirsch and Marie Bianco.

Swordfish

1	cup ripe tomatoes, seeded and finely chopped
	juice of 2 lemons
2	tablespoons olive oil
	puree from caramelized garlic
1	tablespoon dried thyme
1	tablespoon dried mint
1/2	teaspoon Tabasco
	freshly ground black pepper to taste
4	6-ounce swordfish steaks, cut 1/2 inch thick
2	tablespoons butter

Olive Relish

1	cup pitted ripe black olives, chopped
1/2	cup red onion, grilled and chopped
1/2	cup red bell pepper, grilled and chopped
1/4	cup scallions, chopped
1/4	cup pecans or walnuts, chopped
2	tablespoons olive oil
1	tablespoon balsamic vinegar
	puree from 4 cloves caramelized garlic
	freshly ground pepper to taste

For caramelized garlic: Cut a quarter inch off bottom of root end of each head of garlic, brush with olive oil and place on cool edge of grill for about 20 to 30 minutes. Cover garlic with foil and grill for another 20 to 30 minutes until cloves are soft and creamy.

For the olive relish: Combine all the ingredients in a medium bowl and mix well. Allow flavors to blend, unrefrigerated, for an hour.

For swordfish: In a shallow, nonreactive bowl combine the tomatoes, lemon juice, olive oil, garlic, thyme, mint, Tabasco and black pepper. Mix well. Marinate the swordfish steaks in this mixture, refrigerated for an hour. Preheat the grill to medium-high temperature. Remove the swordfish steaks from the marinade and place on the grill for 4 to 5 minutes. Turn and cook for an additional 4 to 5 minutes. Brush the fish occasionally with the marinade. To use the marinade as a sauce, bring it to a boil and stir in butter. Serve with the relish.

Makes 4 servings.

Pea Pods and Jumbo Shrimp

8	ounces pea pods
6	ounces jumbo shrimp, cooked and shelled
2	green onions, thinly sliced
4-6	water chestnuts, thinly sliced

Dressing

4	tablespoons oil
	a dash of sesame oil
1	teaspoon grated fresh ginger
1/2	clove garlic, crushed
	juice and grated rind of half a lemon
	salt and pepper

Trim the pea pods and place in a bowl or casserole with 2 tablespoons salted water. Cover loosely and cook on high for one minute. Allow to cool and combine with the shrimp, water chestnuts and green onions. Mix with the dressing ingredients and place on serving dishes. Reheat thoroughly on high for one minute before serving.

Irene Kaufman's Island Shrimp with Black Bean Salsa and Roasted Red Pepper Hummus

40	large shrimp (can use more)
2	tablespoons chopped parsley
2	tablespoons chopped cilantro
2	cloves crushed garlic
1/2	lemon, juiced
2	tablespoons semi-dry sherry
2	tablespoons virgin olive oil
1/2	teaspoon hot Hungarian paprika
1/2	teaspoon sea salt
1/4	teaspoon ground mace
1	teaspoon freshly ground black pepper
1	pinch saffron
	Sunbean Salsa* Black Bean Dip
	Caribbean Chick* Roasted Red Pepper Hummus

Shell and devein shrimp. Rinse. Mix remaining ingredients in a large bowl. Add shrimp, cover and refrigerate overnight. Oil the grill grate and pre-heat. Drain shrimp and grill about 5 minutes. Spoon "Sunbean Salsa" on 1/2 side of each plate. Spoon "Caribbean Chick" on 1/2 plate next to black bean salsa. Divide the shrimp into 8 portions and arrange in center of the plate over black beans and the red pepper hummus. Garnish with fresh cilantro sprigs.

*Products by Irene's Cuisine

Shrimp Victoria

2	pounds shrimp, cleaned and deveined
1	pound mushrooms or 2 small jars button mushrooms, sliced
1/2	cup onion, chopped
1/4	cup butter
2	tablespoons flour
1	teaspoon salt
	dash freshly ground pepper
3	cups sour cream
	dry white wine (optional)
	white rice

Sauté the onion in butter until wilted. Add mushrooms, and cook 2 minutes. Then add shrimp. Cook another 4 minutes, stirring. Add the flour, salt, pepper and sour cream. Cook gently, stirring until heated. Thin with dry white wine, if necessary. Serve over rice.

Serves 6.

Pan-Fried Great Lake Smelts

2	pounds smelts
1/2	cup flour
1/4	cup finely ground almonds
1/2	teaspoon salt
1/2	teaspoon pepper
1/4	pound butter (one stick)
	lemon wedges
	beer

Thoroughly clean the smelts but leave the head intact. Wash and pat each smelt dry. Place them in a large bowl and pour enough beer to cover. Marinate in refrigerate for 2 hours.

Remove smelt from beer and pat dry.

In a large bowl combine flour, ground almonds, salt and pepper. Dredge the smelts, one at a time, in this until lightly coated.

Melt the butter in a deep heavy skillet. When hot, add smelt split-side down. Fry as many fish as will fit into the skillet comfortably. Turn the fish and brown the skin side. Fry until crisp. Add more butter if necessary.

Drain briefly on paper towels and serve with lemon wedges.

59

Seafood Caper Pasta

24	medium shrimp, or 16 medium scallops
2	tablespoons olive oil
2	medium onions
2	cloves garlic, minced
1/2	cup sliced mushrooms
1/4	teaspoon ground red pepper, cayenne
2	tablespoons fresh basil, chopped
3	14-ounce cans whole tomatoes
1	4-ounce can tomato paste
2	tablespoons capers

Using half of the olive oil, sauté the shrimp or scallops with half of the onion and garlic, then set aside.

Sauté the remaining onion and garlic using the remaining olive oil. Add the tomatoes, pepper, mushrooms, capers and basil. Bring to a boil, then add the tomato paste and simmer for 20 minutes. Add the shrimp or scallops and simmer for 5 more minutes. Serve over pasta.

Make 4 servings.

Risotto con Gamberi for Two

6	jumbo shrimp, peeled
1	tablespoon olive oil
1	tablespoon butter or margarine
1	onion, chopped
1	clove garlic, minced
1/2	cup arborio rice
14	ounces chicken broth to taste
1/4	cup Parmesan cheese

First, lightly brush shrimp with olive oil and grill or broil on both sides. Heat the olive oil and butter or margarine together in a heavy saucepan. Add onion and cook over medium heat until soft and golden. Then add garlic and rice and stir for about 3 minutes. Next add 3/4 cup broth and reduce heat to low. Cover and simmer for 5 to 8 minutes or until most of the liquid has been absorbed. Add remaining broth in 2 additions. Cook about 20 minutes, add salt to taste. Remove from heat and add the shrimp and half the cheese. Stir with a fork. Top with remaining cheese and serve.

Makes 2 to 3 servings.

Poultry & Game Main Dishes

Chicken with Mushrooms and Grapes

1	tablespoon flour
1/4	teaspoon salt (optional)
1/4	teaspoon pepper
2	pounds boneless chicken breast, skinned and cut into large pieces
2	tablespoons oil or margarine
1/4	cup onion, minced
1/4-1/2	pound fresh mushrooms
3/4	cup chicken broth
1/2	cup white wine
1/2	cup 1 percent milk
1	tablespoon cornstarch
1	tablespoon water
1	cup seedless grapes

Preheat oven to 325°. In a bag combine flour, salt and pepper. Shake chicken in a bag to coat. Heat margarine in a skillet and add chicken. Sauté until light brown and then place in a casserole. Add onion to skillet and cook until tender. Add mushrooms. Cook for 3 minutes, and spoon onions and mushrooms over chicken in casserole. Add broth and wine to skillet. Bring to a boil and add milk. Simmer over medium-high heat for 5 minutes and add cornstarch and water. Stir until thickened. Pour over chicken. Cover casserole and bake for 20 minutes. Add grapes and bake 10 more minutes. Serve immediately. Good with rice. Perfect for a buffet table. It can be made ahead of time without the grapes.

Makes 4 to 6 servings.

Chicken and Herb Loaf

1	pound ground raw chicken
6	tablespoons whole-wheat breadcrumbs
1	small onion, grated
1	clove garlic, peeled and crushed
2	tablespoons chopped parsley
1	tablespoon chopped fresh thyme
1	medium parsnip, peeled and grated
2	eggs, beaten
	salt and freshly ground pepper

Garnish

	a little olive oil
1	tablespoon chopped parsley
	sprigs of fresh rosemary

Mix the ground chicken with the breadcrumbs, onion, garlic, parsley, thyme, parsnip and beaten eggs. Add salt and pepper to taste. Spoon the mixture into a greased and lined loaf pan. Cover with a piece of greased foil. Bake in the oven for about 50 minutes, until cooked through. Test with a skewer. For a brown top, remove the foil for the last 8 to 10 minutes. While it is still hot, brush the top of the loaf with oil, and sprinkle with the chopped parsley. Carefully take the loaf out of the pan, and serve either hot or cold, garnish with rosemary.

Frogs' Legs

12	large frogs' legs
1/2	cup butter (2 sticks)
2	cloves garlic, crushed
2	tablespoons parsley, chopped
2	tablespoons chives, chopped
1	teaspoon fresh tarragon
2	tablespoon brandy
1/4	cup dry white wine or sherry
	juice of 1/2 lemon
	salt and pepper to taste

Wash the frogs' legs in cold water. Dry well. Season to taste with salt and pepper.

Heat the butter in a large heavy skillet until foamy. Add the garlic, lemon juice and frogs' legs.

Sauté over moderately high heat until legs are golden brown on all sides. Add the parsley, chives and tarragon. Cook for 1 minute.

Increase the heat to high. Pour in the brandy. Heat for 10 seconds and carefully flame. After the flame dies away, reduce the heat and add the wine or sherry and cook for another minute. Serve immediately.

(The Great Lakes abound with frogs. The drumstick section of large chicken wings may be substituted for the frogs' legs.)

Chicken Patrick

4	chicken breasts, skinless, boneless
	pepper, ground black
1	green pepper, chopped
6	ounces pineapple chunks
1	white onion, diced
2	cloves garlic, diced
	rice or noodles

Sauce

8	ounces tomato sauce
1	tablespoon horseradish
	a couple shakes Worcestershire sauce
4-5	drops Tabasco sauce

For sauce: Combine ingredients.

Meanwhile, wilt onions and garlic in oil. In a heavy saucepan, add chicken and salt and pepper to taste and brown for 6 to 10 minutes. Pour sauce over chicken and simmer for 20 minutes. Add green pepper and pineapple. If needed to thin sauce, add pineapple juice. Simmer 10 more minutes.

Serve over rice or noodles.

Makes 4 servings.

Jeff Smith's Fricassee of Rabbit or Chicken

From Jeff Smith's The Frugal Gourmet Cooks American.

2	rabbits, about 3 pounds each, skinned and cut up, or similar amount of chicken
4	egg yolks, beaten
2	cups bread crumbs
1/8	teaspoon mace
1/8	teaspoon nutmeg
1/4	cup butter or olive oil for frying
2	cups brown gravy
1	glass, about 1 cup, red wine
1/2	pound fresh mushrooms, sliced
	salt to taste
2	tablespoons butter and 2 tablespoons flour, cooked together to form a roux

Add mace and nutmeg to the bread crumbs. Rub the rabbit or chicken pieces with the egg yolks and roll in bread crumbs. Fry in butter or oil in a black frying pan or Dutch oven until well browned. Add the remaining ingredients and stir until thick. Cover and simmer until tender.

Veal Shank
by Chef George Kamilaris
Georgio's Cafe International
426 N. Superior Street
Toledo, Ohio 43604
See Page 89

Phyllo Garlic Chicken

6	sheets phyllo
1/4	pound melted butter
6	garlic cloves, slivered
	lemon pepper
6	skinned chicken breasts

Brush phyllo sheets with butter and fold in half lengthwise. Sprinkle lemon pepper over chicken breasts, and add one slivered clove of garlic at the bottom of each phyllo sheet. Wrap the chicken breasts in the phyllo, folding the sheets of phyllo as you would an American flag, into a triangular shape. Place in a cooking pan and bake for 1 hour in a preheated 350° oven.

Greek Feta Chicken

1 1/2	cups plain low-fat yogurt
1	large clove garlic, chopped fine
1/4	teaspoon pepper
2 to 3	teaspoons fresh or 1/2 teaspoon dried oregano, chopped
4	boneless, skinless chicken breast halves
1/2-3/4	cup feta cheese
	parsley

Combine the first four ingredients in a flat bowl. Add the chicken pieces and turn to coat. Let stand for at least 45 minutes. Remove chicken from marinade and grill or broil about 6 to 7 minutes per side or until chicken is done. Do not overcook. Top with crumbled feta cheese and heat until cheese is soft. Garnish with marinade.

Herbed Chicken with Wine and Cream Sauce

2	tablespoons oil, divided
1	medium onion, sliced thin
1	cup sliced mushrooms
3	pounds deboned chicken breasts
1/4	cup flour
	salt and pepper
1	teaspoon dried tarragon
1	cup dry white wine
1/4	cup cream

Heat one tablespoon of oil in a large, heavy skillet. Sauté onion and mushrooms over medium-high heat for 4 to 5 minutes, or until softened, but not brown.

While the vegetables are cooking, skin chicken. Place flour in a shallow bowl and stir in a sprinkling of salt and pepper. Dredge chicken pieces in flour mixture. When veggies are softened, add remaining tablespoon of oil to skillet and add chicken pieces, pushing veggies to the sides. Sauté chicken for 3 minutes on each side. Sprinkle tarragon over chicken. Season with salt and pepper. Add wine and stir, scraping browned bits from the bottom of the pan.

Cover and simmer over low heat for 30 minutes or until the chicken is tender. Remove chicken pieces to a serving dish. Turn heat to high. Add cream and boil rapidly, stirring, for 2 minutes until sauce thickens. Pour over chicken.

Serves 4.

Broiled Chicken in Lemon Juice and Oregano

6 to 8	pieces chicken
1/2	cup olive oil
	juice of 2 lemons
1/4	cup oregano
	salt and pepper to taste

Rinse the chicken pieces and pat dry. In a bowl, make a marinade by combining olive oil with lemon juice and oregano. Dip each piece of chicken in marinade. Season with salt and pepper. Marinade for several hours or overnight.

In a preheated broiler, place the chicken and broil 6 inch from the heat for about 15 minutes, or until brown, basting frequently. Turn once, broil until done.

Company Chicken

8	chicken breasts, skinned and boned
1	8-ounce package creamed cheese
1/2	cup finely chopped green onions, including stems
	salt to taste
16	strips bacon

Cover chicken breasts with wax paper and pound thin. Divide cream cheese into 1 ounce balls and roll in chopped onion.

Salt chicken and place onion covered cream cheese ball in center of each piece. Wrap chicken around cheese and wrap with 2 slices of bacon so that cheese is completely sealed inside. One slice of bacon can be used if wrapped carefully.

Bake at 350° for 35 to 45 minutes until tender. It can be made up to two days in advance.

Serves 4 to 8.

Thymely Creations' Smoked Turkey Linguine

Shelly Moore owns Thymely Creations, a Personal Chef Service, in Toledo.

7	ounces fresh green beans
1/2	pound smoked turkey breast, Julienne sliced
1	14 1/2-ounce can stewed tomatoes
4	ounces shredded Monterey Jack cheese
1	2 1/4-ounce can sliced black olives
2	green onions, sliced
1/2	cup grated Parmesan cheese
1	package prepared Good Seasons Italian dressing
5	ounces cooked, fresh linguine (not dried)

Toss together cooked linguine, green beans, stewed tomatoes, turkey, Monterey Jack cheese, Parmesan cheese, green onions and olives in a large bowl. Pour prepared Good Seasons dressing over all ingredients and toss thoroughly. Serve at room temperature.

Town Square, Lima, Ohio

University Of Toledo

Creamy Chicken Cacciatore

2 to 3	pound broiler-fryer chicken pieces
1	large onion, sliced and separated into rings
2	tablespoons butter
1	cup chopped tomato
1	cup green pepper strips
1/2	cup milk
1 1/2	teaspoon oregano
1/2	teaspoon pepper
1/2	pound Velveeta cheese, cubed

Brown the chicken with onion on all sides in butter in a large skillet. Add tomatoes, green peppers, milk and seasonings. Bring to a boil. Reduce heat, cover and simmer for 20 minutes or until chicken is tender. Uncover. Continue cooking for 10 minutes. Remove chicken to platter. Keep warm.

Stir in Velveeta cheese cubes in a skillet until melted. Serve over chicken.

Serves 4.

Elizabeth Barry's Summer Chicken

A simple and succulent dish of golden chicken with an exciting aroma, reminiscent of a Middle Eastern feast. Send a child out into the garden to pick handfuls of fresh mint.

6	chicken breasts
1	lemon, juice only (bottled will do)
2-3	tablespoons olive oil
2	cloves garlic, crushed
1	teaspoon ground turmeric
2-3	teaspoons ground cumin
1	teaspoon salt
	few grinds black pepper
	those mint leaves
	soft, plain, natural yogurt or yogurt cheese
1	jar Ginger Jar Apricot and Green Ginger Chutney

Mix everything but the chicken in a large, shallow dish. Smear the mixture on the chicken breasts and leave to marinate for an hour or so at room temperature.

Half an hour before serving, cover dish with foil or lid and cook at 350° for about 1/2 hour. Test for doneness with a skewer.

To serve, spoon yogurt or yogurt cheese on top and serve with Ginger Jar Apricot and Green Ginger Chutney!

Note: If you prefer to use chicken on the bone, increase the cooking time to about 1 1/4-1 1/2 hours.

Mallard Duck with Turnip Stew

1	mallard duck, jointed
	oil or butter for frying
1	tablespoon flour
1	medium onion, finely chopped
2	cloves garlic, finely chopped
	salt and pepper to taste
	water or light stock
5	medium turnips, quartered
1/2	cup coarsely chopped scallion greens

Cut duck into quarters.

In a large heavy skillet, heat about 2 teaspoons of oil or butter. Add duck and sauté until brown on both sides, about 6 to 8 minutes. Remove the duck and set aside.

Add the flour to the fat and stir until it forms a dark thick roux.

Add the onion, garlic, salt and pepper. Mix well. Return the pieces of duck to the skillet and add enough water or stock to cover.

Cover the skillet and simmer 1 hour. Add the turnips and scallion greens and simmer until tender, about 35 minutes.

Roast Wild Duck

2	wild ducks
	salt
1	onion, halved
1	apple, halved
1	stalk celery, chopped
2	sprigs parsley
1/4	cup olive oil
1/4	cup sweet vermouth

Preheat the oven to 475°.

Thoroughly clean and wash the ducks. Pat dry. Rub inside and out with salt. Stuff each duck with half the onion and apple, several pieces of celery and 1 sprig of parsley. Sew the ducks closed.

Combine olive oil and vermouth.

Place the ducks on a roasting rack in a shallow pan and roast for 20 to 25 minutes per pound. Baste the duck every 10 minutes with the olive oil and vermouth combination.

Remove the duck from the oven. Remove the thread. Quarter or halve the ducks and serve.

Roast Rock Cornish Hens

6	frozen cornish hens
6	peeled cloves garlic
3	tablespoons dried tarragon
3/4	cup dry white wine
3/4	cup butter
1 1/2	teaspoon salt
3/4	teaspoon pepper
	garlic salt

The day before, thaw the hens in a refrigerator. Early in the day, make a basting sauce with the melted butter, wine and a tablespoon tarragon. In each hen place one clove garlic, 1 teaspoon tarragon, 1/4 teaspoon salt, 1/8 teaspoon pepper. Sprinkle liberally with garlic salt. One hour before serving, start heating the oven to 450°. In a large shallow open pan without a rack, bake the hens 45 minutes until brown. Baste several times while roasting.

Makes 6 servings.

Ft. Meigs, Perrysburg

577
Foundation,
Perrysburg

Chicken Divan

4	chicken breasts, skinned and deboned
1	10-ounce package frozen chopped broccoli
1	can cream of chicken soup
1/2	cup mayonnaise
1/2	teaspoon lemon juice
1/2	teaspoon curry
1/2	cup cheddar cheese, shredded
1/2	cup bread crumbs

Debone chicken and place in a greased casserole. Sprinkle the broccoli over chicken. Combine soup, mayonnaise, lemon juice and curry, and pour over broccoli. Sprinkle top with cheddar cheese and bread crumbs. Bake at 350° for 40 to 50 minutes.

Turkey Barbecue

1	10 to 12 pound fresh turkey
1/2	cup melted butter or margarine
1/2	cup olive oil
2	cups cider vinegar
1	cup tomato sauce
1/2	cup Worcestershire sauce
1/3	cup fresh squeezed lemon juice
2	tablespoons dry mustard
3	tablespoons cumin powder
2	teaspoons white pepper
2	teaspoons salt
2	cloves garlic, crushed

Make a hefty charcoal fire. Heat until the coals turn gray.

Thoroughly wash and clean the turkey. Gently pat dry.

In a heavy saucepan, combine all of the ingredients. Simmer for 10 minutes.

Brush the inside and outside of the turkey with the sauce.

Insert a spit rod through the turkey tail and diagonally through the breast bone. Secure the turkey with spit prongs. Tie the wings and legs closely to the body with string.

Heap the coals in the back of the firebox or to one side of the grill. Place a piece of aluminum foil in the center to catch the drippings. Place the spit in its holders.

While the turkey rotates on the spit, brush it with the barbecue sauce every 15 minutes. Add more coals as needed to keep the temperature high. Wrap wing and leg ends with foil if they start to brown too quickly.

Barbecue the turkey for roughly 20 minutes per pound. Remove the turkey from the spit and cool for 20 minutes before carving. Serve with the remaining barbecue sauce.

Spaghetti with Chicken Tomato Sauce

1	3 to 4 pound chicken
1	pound spaghetti
1	can Campbell's cream of mushroom soup
2	15-ounce cans Hunt's tomato sauce
2	tablespoons cumin
2	tablespoons chili powder
1	tablespoon celery salt
2 to 3	cups grated mild cheddar cheese
	salt and pepper

Boil chicken in water to cover. Allow to cool enough to handle. Remove meat from bones. Reserve broth. Cook spaghetti in reserved broth to desired tenderness. Place spaghetti in baking dish. Combine soup, sauce and spices in large mixing bowl and add chicken. Stir well and add to spaghetti. Top with 2 to 3 cups grated cheddar cheese. Bake in 350° oven 30 to 40 minutes or until cheese melts.

Makes 6 servings.

Sunburst Stir-Fry

1	20-ounce can chunk pineapple, in juice or syrup
1	chicken breast, split, skinned and boned
2	large cloves garlic, pressed
2	tablespoons minced ginger, or 1 teaspoon ground ginger
2	tablespoons olive oil
2	medium carrots, sliced
1	green bell pepper, slivered
4	ounces thin spaghetti, cooked
3	green onions, chunked

Sauce

1/3	cup reserved pineapple juice
1/3	cup soy sauce
1	tablespoon cornstarch
1	tablespoon sesame oil

Drain pineapple, reserving 1/3 cup for sauce. Cut chicken into chunks. In a large wok, skillet or stir fry pan, stir fry chicken with garlic and ginger in oil for 2 minutes. Add pineapple, carrots and bell pepper. Cover, steam for 2 to 3 minutes until vegetables are tender crisp. Stir in spaghetti. Combine sauce ingredients, pour into pan along with green onions. Toss until all ingredients are mixed thoroughly and heated through.

Makes 4 servings.

Otsego Park on the Maumee River

Bowling Green
State University

Chicken Breasts in Phyllo

1 3/4	cups mayonnaise
1 1/4	cups green onion, chopped
1/3	cup lemon juice
2	cloves garlic, minced
1	tablespoon tarragon, or 12 small tarragon stems fresh
12	chicken breasts, halved, boned and skinned
	salt and pepper
24	sheets phyllo dough
1 3/4	cups butter, melted
1/3	cup freshly grated Parmesan cheese

Combine first 5 ingredients to make sauce. If using fresh tarragon, don't mix into sauce. Just lay the strips on chicken and sauce before wrapping with phyllo. Lightly sprinkle chicken pieces with salt and pepper. Place sheet of phyllo on working surface. Quickly brush with melted butter, about 2 to 3 teaspoons. Place second sheet on top of first. Brush with melted butter. Spread about 1 1/2 tablespoons of sauce on each side of chicken. Place breast in one corner of the buttered phyllo sheets. Fold corners over breast. Then fold sides over, roll breast in sheets to form a package. Place in an ungreased baking dish. Repeat with remaining breasts and phyllo. Brush packets with rest of butter. Sprinkle with Parmesan cheese. At this point, the dish may be tightly sealed and frozen. Thaw completely before baking. Bake at 375° for 20 to 25 minutes or until golden. Serve hot.

Makes 12 servings.

Chicken Moussaka

4	tablespoons olive oil
1	medium onion, finely chopped
1	clove garlic, peeled and crushed
1	pound ground raw chicken
2	tablespoons tomato paste
1 1/4	cups chicken stock
2	tablespoons parsley, chopped
	salt and fresh ground black pepper
2	medium size eggplants, thinly sliced
2/3	cup plain yogurt
1	egg
1/4	cup grated cheese
1	tablespoon grated Parmesan cheese.

Heat half the oil in a pan, and add the chopped onion and garlic and fry gently for 3 minutes. Add the ground chicken and fry until lightly browned. Add the tomato paste, chicken paste and parsley. Salt and pepper to taste. Cover and simmer gently for 15 minutes. Lay the eggplant slices on lightly greased cookie sheets and brush with the remaining olive oil. Bake in the oven for 8 minutes. Arrange a layer of eggplant and then a layer of chicken in a lightly greased ovenproof dish. Repeat the layers, finishing with a layer of eggplant. Beat the yogurt with the egg and grated cheese and spoon evenly over the top. Sprinkle with grated Parmesan cheese. Bake in the oven for 35 to 40 minutes, until the top is bubbling and lightly golden. Serve piping hot.

Chicken Vermouth

6	chicken breasts, halved
1/4	cup oil
1/4	cup soy sauce
3/4	cup dry vermouth
1/4	cup water
1	tablespoon brown sugar
1	tablespoon ginger

Place boneless, skinless chicken breasts in a shallow casserole. Pour the mixed ingredients over the breasts. Bake uncovered in a preheated 375° oven for 1 1/2 hours. The big advantage to this dish is that you do not have to brown the chicken or cover it.

This is good served over rice with tomato aspic.

Makes 6 or 7 servings.

Tokyo Chicken

2 to 3	pounds fryers cut in pieces
	flour
	salt and pepper
	olive oil
1 1/2	cups Japanese soy sauce
4	tablespoons brown sugar
3	tablespoons molasses
3	pints water

Season flour with salt and pepper, place in bag with chicken and shake. Brown lightly in olive oil. Combine soy sauce, brown sugar and molasses. Add to water. As chicken pieces brown, drop them in the simmering liquid and continue to cook about 30 minutes or until they are tender and a shiny ebony color.

Makes 6 servings.

R. Andrew Odum's Thai Curry

R. Andrew Odum is the Curator of the Department of Herpetology at the Toledo Zoological Society.

See picture page 136.

1	pound sliced chicken breast
3	green onions, sliced small
1	green pepper, sliced into slivers
2	carrots, sliced into slivers
6	mushrooms, quartered
4	cloves garlic, diced
1 1/2	tablespoons coriander
1	teaspoon Chile paste, Thai style is preferred
1	tablespoon fish sauce
1	10-ounce can coconut milk
1	tablespoon peanut oil

Heat oil in wok until hot (smoking slightly). Add garlic and stir-fry for 15 seconds. Add chicken and cook until well done (in hot wok, about 1-2 minutes). Add onion, peppers, mushrooms and carrots. Stir-fry 1-2 minutes or until vegetables change to a deep color (do not overcook). Add coconut milk, fish sauce, coriander and Chile paste. Heat to a boil. Serve with rice.

Octagon Barn, Bryan

Chicken a L'Orange

2	cups Stove Top flexible serving stuffing mix
1 1/2	cups orange juice
4	deboned chicken breasts
	flour
2	tablespoons oil
	baby carrots or other vegetables of choice

Combine the stuffing with 3/4 cup orange juice. Let stand, stirring occasionally, about 5 minutes or until the liquid is absorbed.

Top each cutlet with stuffing. Roll up and secure with toothpicks. Roll in flour, shaking off the excess.

Sauté chicken rolls in oil in skillet until lightly browned. Slowly add remaining orange juice. Cover and simmer for 7 minutes. Add vegetables and simmer for an additional 3 minutes.

Lemon Chicken over Pasta

	boneless chicken breasts
	sliced mushrooms
1	tablespoon whipped butter
1	small can chicken broth
	Lawry's seasoned salt
	lemon juice to taste
1 to 2	tablespoons flour
	favorite pasta shape, cooked, kept warm
1	teaspoon minced garlic

Melt the butter in a teflon pan, toss in sliced mushrooms and snip in chicken pieces. (Suggestion: use scissors.) Toss lightly to cook thoroughly, season with Lawry's Seasoned Salt. Add chicken broth and lemon juice. Cook through until chicken is done. Thicken with flour, serve over cooked pasta.

Meat Main Dishes

John D. Wesley's Noisettes of Pork Tenderloin with Root Vegetables in Puff Pasta Served in a Honey Dijon Mustard Espagnole Sauce

Picture on page 7

8	3-ounce noisettes of pork tenderloin wrapped in bacon
4	ounces carrots, julienned
4	ounces onion, julienned
4	ounces rutabaga, julienned
4	ounces parsnips, julienned
4	ounces turnips, julienned
2	tablespoons Dijon mustard
8	ounces veal stock
2	tablespoons honey
3	tablespoons olive oil
6	tablespoons unsalted butter
1	package puff pastry shells

Heat sauté pan with olive oil. Brown pork noisettes. Drain off excess fat. Add julienne vegetables and sauté with pork. Add Dijon mustard, honey and veal stock and bring to a boil. Put pan in 400° oven for 15 minutes. Remove pork and place pan back on burner, reduce sauce. Place noisettes of pork in puff pastry shell. Add unsalted butter to reducing sauce. Salt and pepper to taste. Pour sauce with vegetables over pork in pastry shell. Replace lid on pastry shell.

Ropa Vieja

2	pounds pork or beef stew meat
4	large tomatoes, peeled and chopped
1	medium onion, chopped
3	tablespoons oil
1	clove garlic, minced
1	can jalapeno chilies, sliced thin
1	bay leaf
1	green pepper, sliced
1/2	cup beef broth
1	cup catsup
1	tablespoon juice from chilies
1	tablespoon vinegar
	tortillas or rice

Cook the beef or pork with 1 1/3 cups water and 1 teaspoon salt until shreddable. Shred very finely. Make a sauce of all the tomatoes, onion, garlic, vinegar, bay leaf and green pepper. Fry in oil and cook until some of the juice has cooked down. Add the cooked meat and the other ingredients. Continue to cook until the flavors are well blended.

If served as a hot hors d'oeuvre, it should be dry enough so that it doesn't drip when served with tortillas. If used as a main dish over rice, retain more of the juice.

Serves 15 people as an hors d'oeuvre, or 8 people as a main dish.

Ratatouille Beef Pie

1/3	cup chopped onion
1	pound ground round steak
1	teaspoon salt
1/2	cup water
2	tablespoons olive oil
1/2	cup sliced onion rings
1	medium eggplant, coarsely chopped
1	zucchini, coarsely chopped
2	medium cloves garlic, crushed
1/4	teaspoon pepper
1	teaspoon Italian seasoning
3	plum tomatoes, cut in wedges
1 1/2	cups shredded mozzarella cheese

Preheat oven to 375°. In a bowl, mix the chopped onion, beef, bread crumbs, 1/2 teaspoon salt and 1/4 cup water. Press into 9 inch pie plate, forming a shell with a rim. Bake 22 minutes or until lightly browned. Pour fat from shell.

In a skillet over medium heat, add olive oil, onion rings, eggplant, zucchini and garlic. Sauté for 5 minutes. Add pepper, Italian seasoning and remaining salt and water. Cover 5 minutes to simmer. Add tomatoes and cover 5 minutes.

Spoon mixture into beef shell, cover with cheese and bake 5 to 8 minutes, or until cheese melts.

Serves 5 to 6.

Beef Bourguignonne

3	pounds lean, boneless chuck or round steak, cut into 1-inch cubes
1	large onion, thinly sliced
1	bay leaf
1	clove garlic, crushed
1/2	teaspoon thyme
1	tablespoon parsley, chopped
1/2	teaspoon salt
1/2	teaspoon ground, black pepper
2	tablespoons olive oil
1	cup red wine
18	small, white onions
2	tablespoons flour
1/2	pound mushrooms
1 1/2	cups beef broth or bouillon
2	tablespoons butter

Place meat, onion, thyme, parsley, bay leaf, garlic, salt and pepper in a bowl. Combine olive oil and wine. Pour over beef and marinate 4 hours or more, stirring occasionally. Sauté small white onions until tender. Remove onions from pan.

Dry cubes of beef well and reserve marinade. Sauté beef in hot oil, browning well. Sprinkle on flour, cook a few minutes and pour on marinade and beef bouillon. Bring to a simmer, cover and cook 2 hours.

In the meantime, sauté mushrooms in butter, season beef with salt and pepper, add onions, mushrooms and simmer 15 minutes.

Makes 6 servings.

Note: This is better if prepared one day before serving.

Marinated Pork Chops

1	teaspoon dry mustard
1	teaspoon ginger
1	teaspoon MSG
2	tablespoons molasses
1/2	cup soy sauce
1/4	cup salad oil
	garlic salt or powder
8 to 10	pork chops

Mix the ingredients. Pour into a shallow pan. Place chops in marinada. Marinate for 4 to 6 hours. Turn frequently. Cook over charcoal.

Makes 8 to 10 servings.

New Riegel Style Baked Ribs

2 to 3	boneless country-style porks ribs per person
	Spice Mixture (to taste)
	celery salt
	onion powder
	garlic salt
	salt
	pepper
	paprika

Sauce Mixture

1	32-ounce bottle ketchup
1/3	cup water
1	medium onion, minced
1 1/2	teaspoon salt
1 1/2	teapsoon pepper
1 or 2	cups brown sugar, depending on taste
1/4	cup lemon juice
1	tablespoon dry mustard
3	tablespoon cider vinegar
1	teaspoon garlic powder
3	tablespoon Worcestershire sauce

Prepare the spice mixture. Rub the ribs with cooking oil on all sides, then sprinkle the spice mixture on all sides. Refrigerate until the sauce is ready.

Pour ketchup into a large sauce pan and rinse the bottle with 1/3 cup water and add to pan. Add all other sauce ingredients to the ketchup/water mixture, stir to mix well, and simmer for 30 minutes on medium to low heat, stirring occasionally.

Place ribs in a reheating pan. Carefully pour sauce over all ribs, turning them so that all parts are coated. Sprinkle garlic salt lightly over the ribs and bake uncovered at 350° for 1 1/2 hours.

Stroganoff

1 1/2	pounds round steak, cubed
	oil for frying steak
	salt and pepper
3	cloves garlic
1	24-ounce sour cream
1	can tomato soup
1/2	can mushroom soup
1	teaspoon Worcestershire sauce
	Tabasco sauce, to taste
	noodles or rice
	chopped onion (optional)
	fresh mushrooms (optional)

After frying steak in oil and salt and pepper, drain oil from the pan. Over medium heat, add the rest of the ingredients. Bring to a boil, lower heat and simmer for one hour, stirring frequently. Serve hot over noodles or rice.

Veal Tenderloin Firenze with Risotto

This recipe is from Matthew's Creative Cuisine.

Picture on page 189.

4	pounds veal tenderloin, cleaned and sliced into 1-inch medallions
1	tablespoon butter
1/4	cup pancetta, chopped
1/4	cup chopped shallots
1	large portobello mushroom, julienned
1/2	cup oyster mushrooms
1/2	cup dried cherries
1	cup demi glace
1/2	cup sweet Marsala
2	tablespoons balsamic vinegar
2	tablespoons chopped sage
3	tablespoons chopped parsley
	toasted pine nuts as garnish
	flour for dredging
	olive oil
	salt and pepper to taste

In a sauce pan over medium-high heat, sautéed the pancetta in butter until lightly browned, add shallots and cook for two minutes, stirring occasionally to prevent burning. Add mushrooms, cherries, demi glace, Marsala, balsamic, sage and parsley. Simmer for 20 minutes.

Meanwhile, pat veal dry on paper towels, dredge lightly in flour and sauté in olive oil, Transfer to warm platter and spoon sauce over, sprinkle with toasted pine nuts.

Lazy Day Pot Roast with Nude Noodles

Pot Roast

2	pounds beef pot roast
3	packages Lipton California French Onion Soup Mix and Water

Noodles

8	ounce package wide egg noodles
	boiling water
2	tablespoons butter
1	tablespoon olive oil
1	teaspoon garlic powder
1	teaspoon fine herbs

To prepare the pot roast, place the roast in a dutch oven, and sprinkle it with the soup mix. Barely cover the roast with water. Cover and bake at 350° for 1 hour. Reduce the heat to 325° and continue to bake for 2 more hours.

For the noodles: cook them until they are the desired tenderness. Drain. Melt oil and butter in saucepan and add garlic powder, fine herbs, and salt and pepper to taste. Coat noodles with mixture and serve immediately.

Makes 6 servings.

John Bodner's Chili

1 1/2-2	pounds lean ground beef
1	large green pepper
2	medium to large onions, coarsely chopped
1	15-ounce can dark red kidney beans
1	15-ounce can Brooks Chili Hot Beans
1	quart plain stewed tomatoes
1	4-ounce can mushrooms
3 or 4	garlic cloves, finely chopped, or
1	tablespoon garlic powder
1 or 2	tablespoons chili powder
1	teaspoon cumin
1	teaspoon oregano
1	teaspoon salt, or to taste
1/2	teaspoon black pepper
2	heaping tablespoons of La Victoria Ranchera Salsa (HOT), use less for a milder chili

Cut green pepper into large pieces. Fry meat with onions and green pepper. Add garlic if using fresh in heavy pot. When meat is well browned drain as much grease as possible. Add kidney beans and chili beans. Stir. Add tomatoes. Break tomatoes into small pieces. Stir. Add all spices. Add garlic powder now if not using fresh. Stir. Add Rancher salsa. Stir. Add can of mushrooms. Do not drain. Stir. Simmer for about 1 hour. Stirring occasionally. Chili is better the next day, but is very good "fresh." Do your own thing. Change the spices to your own taste.

Makes 6 to 8 servings.

George A. Kamilaris' Veal Shank

Picture on page 65.

3	pounds sliced veal shanks
1	onion diced
2	tomatoes, sliced
1	bell pepper, diced
1	cup heavy cream
	olive oil
	salt and pepper
	chopped parsley and basil
2-4	ounces flour
	Madiere wine
1	quart veal stock

Sauté veal shanks with olive oil in pan until golden in color. Place in a braising pan.

Sauté onions and garlic. Sprinkle the mixture with flour to thicken. Add the veal stock and bring to a boil. Add the remainder of the ingredients and bring to a second boil. Pour sauce over the veal shanks, and cover the pan. Bake shanks in a 400° oven for 2 hours. Remove sauce and add the heavy cream. Bring to a boil. Reduce heat, and simmer for about 15 minutes.

Pork Roast with Currant Sauce

4-5	pound porkloin roast
2	tablespoon dry mustard
2	teaspoon thyme
1	teaspoon salt
1/2	teaspoon pepper
	garlic powder

Marinade

1	cup sherry
3/4	cup light soy sauce
4	cloves garlic
2	teaspoon ground ginger

Sauce

1	jar currant jelly
1	tablespoon soy sauce
2	tablespoon sherry

Combine mustard, thyme, salt and pepper. Cut small slits about 2 inches apart in roast, shake small amount of garlic powder in each. Rub roast with dry mustard mixture. Combine marinade ingredients. Pour over meat in glass bowl. Refrigerate overnight, turning at least once. Place roast on rack in shallow roasting pan and bake at 325° for 2 1/2 to 3 hours.

For sauce: Melt jelly over low heat, add soy sauce and sherry. Simmer for 2 minutes. Serve with pork roast.

Makes 4 to 6 servings.

Barbecued Ribs

30-35	pounds ribs
10-24	dried serrano chile peppers
6-10	habanero peppers
10-15	ounces sriricha red chili paste
12	ounces Tabasco or Durkee Red Hot Pepper Sauce
10	ounces Melinda's XXX-Hot
5	ounces Jamaica Hellfire 2-in-1 Pepper Sauce
5	ounces Busha Brown's Pukka Hot Pepper Sauce
56	ounces Bullseye Original Barbecue Sauce
56	ounces K.C. Masterpiece Original Barbecue Sauce
72	ounces Kraft Thick and Spicy K.C. Style Sauce
10	cloves crushed garlic
2	tablespoons Luzianne Cajun Spice
1	pound brown sugar

Remove the stems from the dried peppers. Avoid touching the flesh of the peppers are much as possible by wearing rubber gloves or a plastic bag. If your hands do come in contact with the habeneros, be sure to wash them completely and avoid contact with your eyes. Use a blender or a food processor to grind the peppers into powder.

Some of the hot sauces may or may not be available locally, but to achive the desired spiciness, the Melinda's hot sauce is most critical. If substitions are made, be sure to use cayenne, habenero or scotch-bonnet based hot sauces.

Combine all the remaining ingredients, except the ribs, in a large (preferrably non-stick) stock pot. Allow them to simmer for at least one hour on low heat. Simmer the ribs in batches in the sauce for 15 to 20 minutes per batch.

For the marination, cut the ribs into individual pieces. How long you marinate the ribs is a matter of personal choice, but at least overnight is preferrable. Place the ribs in a suitably large sealable container and cover them with sauce to marinated in refrigerator.

After the ribs have been marinated, precook them in a microwave to cut down grilling time. Microwaving time depends on the thickness and type of ribs. For spareribs, allow about a minute per rib, on high. For country-style ribs allow about 1 1/2 minutes per rib, on high.

Grill the ribs on a very low heat for about 10 to 15 minutes again depending upon the thickness. Baste ribs with barbecue sauce at each turning. When the ribs are almost done, they should turn a nice, deep red-brown as the brown sugar carmelizes. Avoid high heat. Dark, burned spots may be helped by added application of the sauce.

Ribs may be grilled ahead of time if desired and then warmed up in the microwave before serving.

This recipe is designed to cook a large batch of ribs for a party, but it can be varied for a smaller, or an even larger batch. Make enough sauce to cover the ribs, usually about 5 ounces per pound of meat.

Baked Brisket

4- 5	pounds flat beef brisket
1/3	cup vinegar
6	dashes soy sauce
	salt and pepper
1/4	cup catsup
1/2	cup brown
4	dashes Worcestershire Sauce

Line broiler pan or flat pan with foil and place the beef in a pan. Salt and pepper well and wrap in foil. Bake at 350° for 1 hour. Reduce heat to 300° and bake for 2 hours. Combine sugar, vinegar, catsup, Worcestershire sauce and soy sauce. Drain grease from brisket. Add the sauce. Wrap foil loosely around meat and cook for 1 hour.

Makes 10 servings.

Note: This brisket is soooo delicious and fork tender. This is a family favorite.

Picnic Roast with Beer Sauce

5	pounds sirloin tip roast
1	16-ounce bottle beer
1/4	cup flour
1/4	teaspoon salt
1/2	teaspoon garlic salt
1/8	teaspoon pepper
1/4	cup salad oil

Marinade

1/2	cup oil
1/4	cup red wine vinegar
1/2	cup tomato puree
1/2	cup marinara sauce
1/4	cup burgundy
1/2	cup sherry
1/2	teaspoon salt
1/4	teaspoon onion salt
1/4	teaspoon garlic salt
1/8	teaspoon pepper

Place roast in a brown-in cooking bag. Add the beer. Bring bag in closely around the roast. Tie with rubber band. Place in bowl. Refrigerate at least 12 hours.

The next day, preheat the oven to 325°. Remove the roast from bag. Reserve beer. Rub roast with spices and flour. Place roast on rack. Cook uncovered for 1 hour and 50 minutes. Basting exactly every 10 to 15 minutes with a quarter cup oil mixed with a half cup beer. Roast is done when thermometer reads 140°, cool.

Make marinade. Slice roast for sandwiches and placed in a large casserole. Pour marinade on meat. Refrigerate covered overnight, or at least for 12 hours.

Makes 10 big sandwiches.

This is especially good when served on dark bread, such as pumpernickel. Very messy.

Cottage Pie

4	chopped steaks
1	large green pepper, chopped
1	large onion, chopped
1	can sliced mushrooms
2	jars mushroom gravy
8	potatoes
1/4	cup skim milk
	salt and pepper
2	cups mozzarella cheese
1/4	cup Parmesan cheese

Brown the chopped steaks in a skillet. Add the green pepper, onions and mushrooms. When cooked through, discard any visible fat and return to the pan. Add gravy and heat. Boil potatoes until fork tender. Mash potatoes with milk, salt and pepper. They should be stiff. Place chopped steaks in bottom of a casserole. Place potatoes on top of meat. Cover pan completely. Add cheeses on top of potatoes and bake at 350° for 20 minutes.

Makes 4 servings.

Pasta Filled Roasted Onion with Veal Slices

2	large sweet onions
8	ounces pasta, cooked
	pesto, commercially prepared or fresh
4	veal cutlets, sliced thin
2	cloves garlic, peeled and finely diced

Pesto

1	large clove garlic, peeled
3	ounces Parmesan, grated
2	cups fresh basil leaves, or Italian parsley leaves, firmly packed
1/4	cup pine nuts
1	cup light olive oil

For pesto: Process until well blended. Refrigerate unused portion.

For onions: Remove skins and bake in an oven at 350° for 1 hour. After cooling, carefully scoop out the inner onion, leaving shell intact, and reserving the inner onion and both tops. Coarsely chop inner onions.

Toss cooked pasta with just enough pesto to coat lightly, and add most of the chopped onion.

Fill the onion shells with pasta mixture, allowing some to cascade out. Top with onion tops.

For veal: Heat olive oil and butter, just enough to coat the bottom of a frying pan. Add 2 garlic cloves, peeled and finely diced. Toss in remainder of cooked onion. Sauté together. Add veal slices, browning lightly, about 2 to 3 minutes, turning once.

Arrange on plates with pasta filled onion. Serve with a hearty Pinot Noir or Merlot. Remember, red wine's flavour is enhanced when served at room temperature, not chilled.

Serves 2.

Penne Salsiccia

1	pound cooked penne
3	cups marinara sauce
1	pound Italian hot sausage, cooked in the skin, cooled, and sliced 1/3 inch thick
1	green pepper, cut into thin strips
1	red pepper, cut into thin strips
1/2	pound fresh spinach, cut in a julienne
3	tablespoons olive oil
1	tablespoons chopped garlic
1/2	cup red wine
1	pound whole milk ricotta

Marinara Sauce

3/4	cup olive oil
1	cup each onion, celery and carrot, diced
1	bunch fresh basil, chopped
4	tablespoons Italian parsley, chopped
2	heads garlic, minced
2	303 cans crushed canned tomatoes
1	cup red wine
12	ounces tomato paste
3	tablespoons sugar
2	tablespoons balsamic vinegar
1	tablespoons salt
1	tablespoon beef base

For marinara sauce: Sauté all veggies in oil until lightly browned. Add the remaining ingredients and simmer 25 to 30 minutes or until veggies are tender. Puree veggies with stab blender or run through a food mill. If too thin, cook a bit longer. If too thick, thin a little with water.

Cook sausages in a cup of water. Prick sausages to release fat. When water evaporates continue cooking until sausage is brown. Remove from pan and drain all grease. Add oil and peppers cooking until tender. Add garlic and cook a few minutes. Add spinach and wine and cook until wilted. Add marinara sauce and sliced sausage. Heat through. Pour over penne and top with ricotta.

Amish Pot Roast

3	pounds beef roast
1	clove garlic, finely minced
1/4	cup soy sauce
1/2	teaspoon dried oregano
1	cup brewed coffee
1	large onion, sliced thin

Preheat oven to 300°. In a heavy sauce-pan, heat some oil on high heat and sear meat on both sides. Remove meat from pan. Add remaining ingredients. Save some onion to place on top of roast. Cover and bake 3 1/2 to 4 hours. Baste often. If needed, add more soy sauce if liquid boils away.

Makes 6 to 8 servings.

Caponata Stuffed Flank Steak

	olive oil
1	tablespoon balsamic vinegar
1/2	medium eggplant, peeled and cubed
2	small or 1 large onion-coarsely chopped
6-8	cloves garlic, minced
1	pound fresh button mushrooms, sliced
3	ounces dried chanterelle, morel or shitake mushrooms
1	can beef broth
1	sweet red pepper, roasted in over, peeled and chopped
1	28 to 32-ounce can plum tomatoes
	salt, pepper, dried marjarom, oregano and basil
	couscous, noodles or rice

Flank Steak

2	pounds flank steak, butterflied
	garlic powder
1/3	cup soy sauce
1	cup red wine

For steak marinade: Mix garlic powder, soy sauce and red wine and marinate steak for 1 to 3 hours. Reserve marinade.

For mushrooms: Place the mushrooms in beef broth in a small sauce pan and bring to a boil and then simmer for about 30 minutes or until the mushrooms are softened. Remove the mushrooms and chop. Strain sand from broth and reserve to add to veggie mixture.

For stuffing: Use about 3 tablespoons olive oil in a large sauté pan over medium heat. Add onion, garlic and eggplant and sauté until soft. Season with salt and pepper. Add rest of veggies and sauté. Add oil as needed. Do not add liquid from tomatoes. Add broth from mushrooms and balsamic vinegar. Cook down until thick and add herbs. Almost all the liquid should be gone when it's done, which should take about 20 minutes.

Lay the flank steak out and spread some of the stuffing on it. Roll up flank steak starting at short end. Tie with string at about 5 places. Place on rack in baking pan. Preheat oven to 425° and place steak in middle rack and cook for 20 minutes. During cooking time baste with marinade until the marinade is gone.

To serve, slice steak and put over couscous, noodles or rice, and serve with cooking juices on the side.

Makes 6 servings.

Chimichangas

2	pounds hamburger
1	onion, chopped
1/3	cup parsley
1 1/2	teaspoon oregano
3/4	teaspoon cumin
1	teaspoon garlic powder
	salt and pepper to taste
1	can refried beans, with peppers
1	can tomato sauce, with tomato bits
1	can pitted ripe olives, chopped
1	cup cheddar cheese
20-24	large flour tortillas, warmed

Cook hamburger with onion and spices. Drain. Add beans, tomatoes, olives and cheese to hamburger mixture.

Put two heaping tablespoons of mixture on edge of each tortilla. Roll up, folding sides as you go. Fry until golden brown. Serve with lettuce, tomatoes, grated cheese and sour cream.

Butterflied Lamb

4	pounds lamb
5	tablespoons oil
	juice and rind of one lemon
	small bunch mint, roughly chopped
	salt and coarsely ground black pepper
1	clove garlic, crushed

To butterfly the lamb, cut through the skin along the line of the main bone down to the bone. Cut the meat away from the bone, opening out the leg while scraping against the bone with a small, sharp knife. Take out the bone and remove excess fat. Flatten thick places by batting with a rolling pin or a meat mallet. Alternatively, make shallow cuts halfway through the thickest parts and press open. Thread two or three long skewers through the meat to make the meat easier to handle and turn on the grill. Place in a plastic bag or large, shallow dish. Mix the other ingredients together and pour over the lamb, rubbing it in well. Cover the dish or seal the bag and leave at room temperature for 6 hours or overnight in the refrigerator. Turn the lamb frequently.

Remove the lamb from the dish or the bag and reserve the marinade. Grill 20 minutes per side for pink lamb and 30 to 40 minutes per side for more well done lamb. Baste frequently during grilling. Remove the skewers and cut the slices across the grain.

Best Ever Meatloaf

3	slices white bread
1	cup skim milk
3/4	pound ground beef
1/4	pound mild sausage
1	egg
1	teaspoon salt
1/2	teaspoon celery salt
3	tablespoons onion, grated
1/4	teaspoon pepper
1/4	teaspoon nutmeg
1/4	teaspoon dry mustard

Soak bread in milk and heat with a wire whisk. Add remaining ingredients in order given. Mix by hand or with spoon, shape into a loaf and place in a loaf pan, lightly brush top of meatloaf with cold water to seal in juices. Bake at 350° for 1 hour.

Makes 4 servings.

Party-Time Barbecued Beef Sandwiches

1	15-ounce can tomato sauce
1/2	cup water
1	cup onion, chopped
1/4	cup green pepper, chopped
2	tablespoon brown sugar, packed
2	tablespoon Worcestershire sauce
1	tablespoon garlic, minced
1 1/2	teaspoon salt
1/4	teaspoon pepper
	few drops Tabasco sauce
2 1/2-3	pounds chuck beef roast
2	tablespoons flour
1/4	cup water
16	hamburger buns or pita halves

Combine the first nine ingredients in a Dutch oven. Trim surplus fat from roast. Place meat in Dutch oven and spoon tomato sauce mixture over it. Bake covered for 4 hours. Remove meat from the Dutch oven mix flour and 1/4 cup water and stir in tomato mixture. On range top, cook over medium heat about 5 minutes or until thickened. Place meat back into sauce and mash with a potato masher. Heat thoroughly and serve on buns or in pitas. Can be kept warm in a slow cooker.

Makes 16 servings.

Mongolian Lamb with Onions

1	pound lean lamb, cut into 1/4 by 2 inch strips
1	egg white
2	cloves garlic, sliced
1/2	teaspoon five spice powder
1/2	inch fresh ginger root, peeled and thinly sliced
1	tablespoon cornstarch
1 1/4	tablespoon light soy sauce
3 1/2	tablespoons rice wine or dry sherry
2	tablespoons water
3	tablespoons cooked oil
6	green onions, chopped

Mix the lamb with the egg white, garlic, five spice powder, ginger root and 1 teaspoon cornstarch and 1 teaspoon soy sauce. Keep on one side. Mix the remaining cornstarch, soy sauce, wine and water together. Heat the wok and add the oil. When it begins to smoke, add the lamb mixture. Reduce the heat and fry for 3 to 4 minutes until the meat browns slightly. Remove or keep on one side. Add the onions and the cornstarch, soy sauce and wine mixture to the wok. Stir until it thickens. Return the meat to the wok and simmer gently for 3 to 4 minutes, or until the meat is tender. Serve as a main dish.

Swiss Ham Ring-Around

1	cup chopped broccoli, un-cooked
2	tablespoons parsley flakes
2	tablespoons onion, finely chopped
2	tablespoons prepared mustard
1	tablespoon butter or margarine, softened
1	teaspoon lemon juice
3/4	cup 3-ounce shredded Swiss cheese
1	can Hormel Chunk Ham, drained and separated into chunks
1	8-ounce can Pillsbury crescent rolls
	grated Parmesan cheese to taste

Preheat oven to 350°. Cook and drain broccoli. Combine parsley, onion, mustard, margarine and lemon juice. Blend well. Add cheese, broccoli and ham. Mix lightly. Set aside. Separate rolls into 8 triangles. On greased cookie sheet, arrange triangles points towards to outside, in a circle with bases overlapping. The center should be open about 3 inches in diameter.

Spoon ham filling in a ring evenly over base of triangles. (Some filling may fall onto cookie sheet. Fold points of triangles over filling and tuck under bases of triangles at center of circle. Sprinkle with Parmesan cheese. Bake at 350° for 25 to 30 minutes or until golden brown. Serve hot.

You can make this up to 3 hours ahead and bake for 30-35 minutes.

Barbecue Lamb Chops

6	loin chops

Marinade

2 1/2	tablespoons wine vinegar
5	tablespoons orange juice
1 1/4	tablespoons tomato sauce
1 1/4	tablespoons brown sugar
1 1/4	tablespoons French mustard
1/2	teaspoon dried tarragon
1 1/4	teaspoons mild curry powder
	salt and freshly ground pepper
1 1/4	teaspoons oil

Blend all the ingredients together for the marinade. Lay the chops in a large shallow dish and pour over the marinade. Cover and chill for at least two hours. Turn the chops over in the marinade, once or twice.

Preheat a large browing dish on full power in a microwave. Put the oil and the drained chops into the dish, pressing the chops against the hot dish. Microwave on roast, for 3 to 4 minutes on each side. Serve immediately.

Stromboli

2	loaves frozen bread dough
1/2	pound cooked salami
1/2	pound cappicola (Italian ham)
1/2	pound provolone cheese
1/2	mozzarella cheese
2	green peppers
2	large onions
4	tomatoes, sliced thin
	salt to taste
	Italian seasoning
	Italian dressing
	margarine

Slice the green peppers and onions thin and sauté. Thaw the 2 loaves of bread and roll them out separately to form large rectangles. Cover both rectangles of bread dough with layers of salami, provolone, sautéd vegetables, tomatoes, cappicola, mozzarella cheese, salt and seasoning. Roll up into a long roll. Pinch edges to seal. Brush with Italian seasoning and/or dressing.

Bake 25 minutes at 400° or until the crust is golden brown. Serve hot or cold, plain or with spiced mustard.

Makes 10 to 15 servings.

Stromboli has become our family's traditional Christmas Eve supper fare.

Mixed Meat Loaf

Meat Loaf

1	clove garlic
6	ounces lean bacon
1	pound ground beef
8	ounces ground pork
6	ounces lambs' liver, finely chopped
6	ounces Canadian bacon, de-rinded and finely chopped
1/2	cup shredded suet
1/2	cup fresh brown bread crumbs
1/2	teaspoon dried oregano
1/2	teaspoon dried herbs
	salt and freshly ground black pepper
4	tablespoons sherry
1	egg, beaten

Glaze

2 1/2	tablespoons apricot jam or marmalade, sieved
1	teaspoon French mustard
1/2	teaspoon meat and vegetable extract

Rub a 2-quart microwaveable loaf pan with the clove of garlic. Lay the bacon in the meat loaf pan to line the base and sides. In a large mixing bowl, mix the ground beef with the pork, liver, Canadian bacon, suet, breadcrumbs and herbs. Season to taste. Beat together the sherry and the egg; add to the mixture and bind together. Transfer to the prepared loaf pan. Smooth the top. Cover and microwave on Roast, for 27 minutes. Turn the dish 1/2 a turn twice during this time. Allow to stand for 10 minutes. Pour off the excess fat and carefully unmold the loaf.

Mix the ingredients for the glaze together and brush over the top and sides of the meat loaf. Delicious hot or cold.

Chops Balsamica

8	boneless pork cutlets
2	yellow onions, finely diced
2	cloves fresh garlic, crushed and minced
2	cups mushroos, sliced, no stems
2	tablespoons butter
2	tablespoons oil
1	cup balsamic vinegar
	black pepper
	potatoes or white rice

Add half the butter and oil to a warm skillet. Bring the pan to moderate heat, and add the onions and garlic. When the onions are clear and slightly browned, remove and set them aside. Add the balance of the butter and oil. Brown the cutlets. When both sides are browned, remove the cutlets. Deglaze the pan with the vinegar. Turn down the heat to a hot simmer. Add the cutlets in a single layer. Spread the onions across the cutlets. Spread the mushrooms across the top. Sprinkle the whole thing with black pepper, and cover with a heavy lid. Simmer for 40 minutes, or until done. Don't let the pan go dry. Add more vinegar or water. Serve with parsley potatoes or white rice.

Italian Meatballs

2	pounds ground round
3/4	cup Italian bread crumbs
3/4	cup Romano cheese
2	eggs to start, may need more

Small amount each:

	basil
	black pepper
	chopped onion
	chopped green pepper

Dip hands in cold water, mix together all the ingredients and form into small meatballs. Brown lightly, add to sauce for pasta.

Vegetables

Stuffed Spaghetti Squash

1/2	spaghetti squash
1	cup aged cheddar cheese, grated
1	cup zucchini squash, grated
1	cup canned tomato sauce
1	clove garlic, mashed
1/2	teaspoon salt
1/4	teaspoon crumbled basil
2	tablespoons grated Parmesan cheese

Place squash, cut sides down, in a large pot with 2 inches of boiling water. Cover and cook until tender. Remove them from the pot and scrape out the inner shreds with a fork. Reserve the shell. Add cheddar cheese, zucchini, tomato sauce, garlic, salt, pepper and basil. Mix well and pile in shell. Sprinkle with Parmesan cheese. Set in shallow baking pan and bake at 350° for 25 to 30 minutes or until bubbling hot.

Turkey Stuffed Baked Peppers with Raisins and Black Olives

Note: This versatile recipe combines a unique blend of raisins, black olives and bread crumbs with turkey stuffed peppers. The recipe suggests layering the two fillings, but they can be used separately as well.

Raisin and Olive Stuffing

6	large green bell peppers
3	tablespoons olive oil
2	cloves garlic
1/4	cup chopped raisins
6	ripe tomatoes, peeled and chopped
15	large black olives, sliced
1 1/2	cups bread crumbs
2	teaspoons oregano
1/4	cup olive oil (save to brush tops)
	salt and pepper to taste

Turkey Stuffing

1	pound ground turkey
1	slightly beaten egg
4	tablespoons finely chopped onions
2/3	cup tomato sauce
1	cup instant rice
	salt and pepper to taste

For raisin and olive stuffing: Cut the tops off the peppers, and clean out the pulp and seeds. In a large pan, heat the olive oil and sauté the garlic. Stir in tomatoes, cover and cook for approximately 14 minutes. Add raisins, olives, oregano, salt, pepper and bread crumbs. Stir ingredients thoroughly.

For turkey stuffing: Mix all ingredients, including the dry uncooked instant rice.

Stuff the bottom half of cleaned peppers with the turkey stuffing. Fill to top with raisin and olive stuffing. Place in a glass baking dish that has been brushed with olive oil. Liberally brush tops of peppers with olive oil. Cover with aluminum foil. Bake at 350° for 1 hour.

Serves 6.

Creative Gourmet's Braised Eggplant and Peppers

Top toast points with this for an appetizer, or serve as an accompaniment to grilled lamb, fish or chicken.

4	tablespoons olive oil
1	1-pound unpeeled eggplant, cut into 3/4 inch cubes
2	onions, halved and thinly sliced
5	garlic cloves, minced
2	red bell peppers, cored and cut into 1/4 inch strips
1/4	teaspoon ground turmeric
1 1/2	cups diced, canned tomatoes with juices
	pinch sugar
2	tablespoons fresh lemon juice
1	tablespoon chopped, fresh cilantro
	salt and pepper to taste

Heat 2 tablespoons olive oil in large nonstick skillet over medium heat. Add cubed eggplant and sauté until golden, about 5 minutes. Transfer eggplant to plate. Add remaining 2 tablespoons olive oil to same skillet and heat over medium-high heat. Add onions and garlic. Sauté until onions are tender and golden, about 6 minutes.

Add bell peppers and turmeric to skillet and sauté until peppers are almost tender, about 6 minutes.

Add tomatoes with their juices and sugar. Boil until mixture thickens slightly, about 3 minutes. Add eggplant, reduce heat and simmer until vegetables are tender, about 6 minutes longer. Stir in lemon juice. Season to taste with salt and pepper. Transfer to bowl and cool to room temperature. Sprinkle with cilantro.

Note: Can be made up to a day ahead. Cover and refrigerate. Serve at room temperature.

Asparagus Frittata

1 1/2	pounds thin asparagus, trimmed
1/2	pounds thin spaghetti
2	tablespoons olive oil
4	tablespoons butter, softened
1	cup finely diced tomatoes
	Italian Fontina cheese
1/2	cup freshly grated Parmesan cheese
4	large eggs, beaten lightly

Cook asparagus in boiling, salted water about 2 or 3 minutes or until crisp tender. Cool and cut in quarter inch pieces on a diagonal. Cook spaghetti in kettle of boiling salted water until just tender, al dente. Drain spaghetti. In a large bowl, toss spaghetti with oil, a tablespoon butter, asparagus, cheeses and salt and pepper to taste. Add eggs and combine well.

In a 12 inch skillet, melt 3 tablespoons of butter over moderate heat. Add the pasta mixture. Spread pasta with 2 forks evenly in pan. Cook frittata on moderate heat for 3 to 5 minutes. Shift skillet so that a quarter of the frittata is directly over the center of burner. Cook for 3 minutes. Keep shifting until frittata is set. Put a heatproof platter over skillet and invert frittata onto it. Slide frittata browned side up back into skillet. Cook for 5 minutes on moderate heat. Slide onto platter. Cool to room temperature. Serve frittata cut in wedges. Great luncheon dish with fresh fruit salad.

Makes 6 to 8 servings.

Green Garden Medley Vegetable Casserole

1	10-ounce package frozen baby lima beans
1	10-ounce package frozen peas
1	10-ounce package frozen cut green beans
1/4	cup green onion, chopped
2	tablespoons butter
1/2	cup mayonnaise
	salt and pepper
1	tablespoon flour
1/2	cup sour cream
1/2	teaspoon crushed basil leaves
3/4	cup shredded sharp cheddar cheese

Place peas in colander and rinse in hot water until thawed. Set aside. Cook the lima beans and green beans per package directions. Drain, rinse in cold water, drain again. Do not overcook.

Melt butter in a skillet. Sauté the onions until soft. Add flour to make a roux. Remove from heat. Add the sour cream, mayonnaise, basil, salt and pepper. Mix well. Combine this mixture with the vegetables.

Place in a buttered 1 1/2 quart casserole. Sprinkle cheese over top. Bake uncovered at 325° for 1/2 hour. Serve hot.

Tomatoes Rockefeller

12	thick tomato slices
1	10-ounce package frozen, chopped spinach.
1	cup soft bread crumbs
1-1 1/2	cups finely chopped green onions
6	eggs, slightly beaten
3/4	cup melted butter or margarine
1/2	cup grated Parmesan cheese
1/2	teaspoon minced garlic
1	teaspoon salt
1	teaspoon thyme
	hot sauce, such as Tabasco, to taste

Arrange tomato slices in a lightly greased 13 by 9 by 2 inch baking pan and set aside.

Cook spinach, drain well and squeeze to remove excess water. Add the remaining ingredients, stirring well. Mound mixture on tomato slices. Bake at 350° for 15 minutes or until set. Sprinkle with additional cheese.

Makes 12 servings.

The General's Potato Pancakes

2	cups finely grated raw potatoes
2	fresh eggs, well beaten
1	tablespoon flour
1/2	teaspoon salt
1/2	teaspoon baking powder
	canola oil

Mix all ingredients together. Fry in small patties until golden brown using canola oil (0% sodium and cholesterol). Add salt to taste.

Broccoli Puff

2	pounds broccoli or asparagus, zucchini or green beans
1/2	cup bread crumbs
1/2	cup grated Parmesan cheese
2	tablespoons melted butter
2	whole eggs
1/2-3/4	cup cream

Boil broccoli in water with one chicken bouillon cube, a pinch of baking soda and 1/4 peeled onion until just tender. Drain, and transfer to a food processor with a steel blade. Puree. Add bread crumbs, cheese, eggs, butter and cream blend once more. Pour into greased souffle dish and bake in 350° oven for a half hour.

Kartoffeln und Gloess (Potatoes and Dumplings)

3	potatoes
2	cups flour
2	eggs
1	teaspoon salt
	chopped onion

Peel potatoes, cut into small pieces and put into kettle of boiling water, to which salt has been added. While potatoes are cooking, mix flour, eggs, salt and enough water to make a soft dough. When potatoes are tender, drop the dough from a tablespoon into the boiling water and cook until the dumplings float on top.

Pour off water and fry dumplings in shortening to which chopped onion has been added. When dumplings are lightly brown, serve with the potatoes.

May be served with navy beans. Also very good with cooked, sweetened blackberries. Dumplings may also be served without frying by lightly frying chopped onion in fat or oil. Pour onion over dumplings and season with sweet cream.

Sugared Asparagus

3	tablespoons butter or margarine
2	tablespoons brown sugar
2	pounds fresh asparagus, cut into 2-inch pieces.
1	cup chicken broth

In a skillet, heat the brown sugar and butter until the sugar is dissolved. Add asparagus and sauté for 2 minutes. Add chicken broth and bring to a boil. Reduce the heat, cover and simmer about 8 minutes or until the asparagus is tender. Remove asparagus to a serving bowl. Cook sauce in pan until it is thick and then pour over the asparagus.

Makes 4 to 6 servings.

Stewed Tomato Casserole

1	large can stewed tomatoes, or if canned whole tomatoes are used, mash them with a fork
1	cup commercial bread crumbs or crumbs from 4 slices of wheat or white bread
2	tablespoons butter or margarine
1	cup sugar
1	teaspoon cinnamon

Cook tomatoes about 3 minutes on medium heat on top of the stove, adding sugar and butter or margarine. Remove from heat and add cinnamon and bread crumbs. Pour into a casserole dish. Bake in a 350° oven for 30 minutes.

Serves 12.

Tangy Cucumber Ring

3	cups grated, peeled cucumber, drained
1/8	teaspoons white pepper
3/4	teaspoon salt
4	cups sour cream
3	tablespoons cider vinegar
3	tablespoons lemon juice
1 1/2	tablespoons sugar
1 1/2	tablespoons chopped chives or green onion
3	envelopes unflavored gelatin
3/4	cup cold water

Sprinkle salt and pepper over cucumbers. Combine sour cream, cider vinegar, lemon juice, sugar and chives or green onions. Sprinkle gelatin over water, let soften. Place the cold water with gelatin over hot water to dissolve. Stir gelatin and cucumbers into sour cream mixture. Refrigerate at least 4 hours.

Makes 8 servings.

Apricot-Pecan Sweet Potatoes

4	large sweet potatoes
1	cup apricot nectar
2	teaspoons grated orange peel
1/2	teaspoon ginger
1	cup brown sugar
1/4	cup butter
1/2	teaspoon cinnamon
1	cup whole pecans

Cook sweet potatoes until tender. Cool, peel and cut into one-inch slices. Set aside.

In a medium saucepan, bring sugar, nectar, butter, peel and spices to a boil and continue for two minutes.

Arrange potatoes in a baking dish, pour sauce over, and arrange pecans on top. Bake at 350° for 30 minutes.

Turnip Souffle

	turnips, washed and peeled
2	tablespoons flour
1	cup (or less) sugar
2	sticks butter, melted
	salt
	white pepper
2	cups half and half
	Ritz crackers, crushed finely

Cook turnips and drain well. Mash through sieve. Mix with flour and sugar. Stir in butter. Add salt and pepper to taste. Mix and season with half and half. Grease a casserole dish. Pour in turnip mixture and add crumbs with a small amount of butter left over from the turnip mixture. Bake at 325° or 350° about 30 minutes.

Barbequed Lima Beans

1	pound dried, baby lima beans
4	cups water
1 1/2	cups chopped onion
1	cup dark brown sugar, packed
1	cup ketchup
2/3	cup dark corn syrup
1	tablespoon salt
1	tablespoon liquid smoke
9	drops Tabasco sauce
	bacon strips, if desired

Wash beans and soak overnight in water in a Dutch oven. DO NOT DRAIN. Add onion. Bring to a boil. Cover and simmer 25 to 30 minutes or until beans are almost tender. Drain and save the liquid. Combine brown sugar, ketchup, corn syrup, salt, liquid smoke and Tabasco sauce in a bowl. Mix well and stir into beans.

Pour into bean pot and bake at 250° for at least 2 hours. Top with bacon strips before baking. Bake uncovered until hot and bubbly.

Makes 9 cups.

Beans, Beans and More Beans

1	16-ounce can kidney beans, drained
1	16-ounce can green beans, drained
1	14-ounce can lima beans, drained
1	20 3/4 ounce can pork and beans
1	cup chili sauce
1	cup brown sugar
1/2	tablespoon mustard
1/2	cup minced onion
1/2	pound smoked and crumbled bacon

In a 2 1/2 quart microwaveable dish combine all the ingredients. Mix very well. Microwave on full power for 16 minutes or until hot and bubbly.

Makes 8 servings.

Eggplant Bake

3	large eggplants
2 1/2	teaspoons salt
	malt vinegar
2 1/2	tablespoons oil
2	large onions, peeled and sliced
2	green chilies, chopped
15	ounces peeled tomatoes, chopped
3/4	teaspoon chili powder
1 1/4	teaspoons crushed garlic
3/4	teaspoon ground tumeric
	oil for deep frying
1/3	cup plain yogurt
1 1/4	teaspoons freshly ground black pepper
4	tomatoes, sliced
2	cups cheddar cheese, grated

Cut the eggplant into quarter inch thick slices. Lay in a shallow dish. Sprinkle with 1 1/4 teaspoon salt and add sufficient malt vinegar to cover. Allow to marinate for 20 to 30 minutes. Drain well. Heat 2 1/2 tablespoons oil in a heavy frying pan and fry the onions until golden brown. Add the chilies, chopped tomatoes, remaining salt, chili powder, garlic and tumeric. Mix well and simmer for 5 to 7 minutes. Remove from heat. Cool and blend to a smooth sauce. Heat the oil for deep frying. Deep fry the drained, marinated eggplant until brown on both sides (2 to 3 minutes on each side). Drain well on a paper towel. Grease a large deep baking dish. Arrange half the fried eggplant rounds closely together in the dish.

Spoon over half the tomato mixture and beaten yogurt. Season with pepper. Add the remaining eggplant rounds and the rest of the tomato sauce and yogurt. Cover with slices of tomatoes and grated cheese. Bake at 350° for 10 to 15 minutes, or until the cheese melts and turns brown. Serve hot as a side dish, or as a main course with pita bread.

California Crescent Vegetable Pie

1	pound ground beef or turkey
1/2	cup chopped onion
3/4	teaspoon salt
1/8	teaspoon pepper
1 1/2	cups sliced zucchini
1/4	cup chopped green pepper
1	teaspoon dill weed
2	tablespoons margarine
8	ounce can Pillsbury crescent rolls
6	ounces or 1 1/2 cup shredded cheddar cheese
1 1/2	tomatoes, sliced

Heat oven to 375°. In a large skillet brown the beef or turkey and onion. Drain. Stir in the 1/2 teaspoon salt and pepper. In another skillet, sauté the zucchini and green pepper in margarine for approximately 5 minutes. Stir in the dill weed and 1/4 teaspoon salt. Separate dough into 8 triangles. Place triangles in the ungreased 8 or 9 inch pie pan. Press over bottom and up sides to form a crust. Combine 1 cup cheese with the meat mixture. Spoon over crust. Spread zucchini mixture evenly over the meat. Top with tomato slices. Bake at 375° for 10 minutes. Sprinkle remaining cheese over tomatoes. Return to oven and bake for an additional 15 minutes. Cool for 5 minutes.

Makes 6 servings.

Garlic Vegetables

2	tablespoons olive oil
1	whole clove garlic, crushed
1	small eggplant
2	small zucchini
	broccoli, chopped
	baby carrots
	mushrooms
1	onion, quartered
	green pepper, sliced
	green beans
1	can stewed tomatoes
1	tablespoon basil
	couscous or angel hair pasta

Optional

	capers
	olives shallots

Parboil baby carrots. Sauté garlic in olive oil. Add onion, green peppers and vegetables, cut into bite-sized pieces. Add stewed tomatoes and basil. Cover pan, and then stir a few times while cooking for about 45 minutes. Serve on a bed of couscous or angel hair pasta.

Makes 4 to 6 servings.

Tomato Pie

9	inch pie shell
	fresh or canned plum tomatoes
1	cup sharp cheddar cheese
3/4	cup Hellmann's mayonnaise
1	medium or large onion, chopped
	optional, lots of fresh basil, either whole or chopped

Bake pie shell at 400° for 10 minutes. Peel and slice tomatoes into shell. The size of the tomatoes will dictate how many are needed. Mix together the cheese, mayonnaise and onion. Spread over the tomatoes. Bake at 350° about 20 minutes until it is brown and bubbly.

Makes 6 to 8 servings.

Corn Souffle Casserole

1/2	pound butter
2	eggs, slightly beaten
1	16-ounce can cream-style corn
1	16-ounce can whole kernel corn, including liquid
2	boxes Jiffy corn muffin mix
1	pint sour cream

Melt the butter and combine the eggs, cream style and whole kernel corn and corn muffin mix. Fold in the sour cream. Spread into a 9 by 13 inch pan, greased with cooking spray. Bake at 375° for 30 to 40 minutes or until the top is golden brown, and a toothpick inserted in the center comes out clean. Cut into 24 squares. Serve hot or at room temperature. Can be reheated.

Serves 12 generously.

Note: this recipe divides in half perfectly.

Curry-Ginger Cooked Cabbage

1	tablespoon butter
1	medium head cabbage, coarsely sliced
1/2	cup water
2	tablespoons Wyler's dried chicken bouillon
2 or 3	teaspoons curry powder
2	teaspoons powdered ginger
	pepper to taste
2 or 3	tablespoons McCormick dried soup greens

Melt butter in an extra large teflon frying pan. Add cabbage. Sauté on low until the cabbage is slightly softened. Mix bouillon in water and add to the cabbage. Simmer on low heat, stirring often, for 5 minutes. Sprinkle curry powder over the cabbage. Stir well. Sprinkle ground ginger over the cabbage. Stir well. Add the dried soup greens. Stir well. Cover and cook on very low heat until the cabbage is done and the soup greens are re-hydrated. Pepper to taste. Keeps well on very low heat and flavor improves.

Makes 4 generous servings.

Broccoli Noodle Pudding

1	16-ounce package wide noodles
2	10-ounce packages frozen chopped broccoli
1 1/4	sticks melted margarine
6	eggs
2	envelopes dry onion soup mix
1	16-ounce carton frozen Coffee Rich

Cook noodles according to package directions. Drain. Add broccoli and melted margarine. Put this into a greased 9 by 13 inch pyrex baking dish.

With hand mixer or blender, combine with eggs, onion soup mix and Coffee Rich.

Pour liquid mixture over noodle mixture. Pierce with fork to allow liquid to penetrate.

Bake at 325° for 1 hour or until top is golden brown.

Makes 8 to 12 servings.

Marinated Tomatoes

sliced tomatoes
celery
green peppers
green onions
Jane's Crazy Salt
Lawrey's Seasoned Salt
coarse ground black pepper
Wishbone Italian dressing

Slice tomatoes. Arrange in pyrex baking dish. Dice celery, green peppers and green onions. Spread diced vegetables over tomatoes. Sprinkle with seasonings. Drizzle with enough Italian dressing to moisten thoroughly. Cover dish with plastic wrap and refrigerate for several hours before serving.

Carrot Sweetmeat

2	ounces olive oil
1	pound carrots, shredded
1/4	teaspoon ground cardamom, crushed
1/4	teaspoon cardamom powder
3/4	cup sugar
1/2	cup hot water
1 1/2	cups milk
5	tablespoons dried milk powder
2	tablespoons slivered almonds or pistachios

Heat oil in a pan, and add carrots. Cook uncovered over medium heat, stirring. Cover and turn heat very low. Cook until carrots are soft. While carrots are cooking make a syrup of sugar and water. Boil until oil level. Add milk, milk powder and cardamom. Stir ingredients and cook on medium until mixture comes away from the pan in one mass. Cool and decorate with almonds and pistachios.

Serves 8.

111

Acorn Squash with Rum Butter Glaze

4	large acorn squash
1/2	cup butter (2 sticks)
2/3	cup water
1/2	cup spiced rum
1	cup firmly packed dark brown sugar
	grated rind of 1 large orange

Preheat oven to 350°.

Trim the ends of the squash. Cut each squash into 4 cross-wise rings. Remove the seeds.

Place the rings side-by-side in buttered shallow baking pans. Add 1/3 cup of water to each pan. Cover with foil and place in the oven for 40 to 45 minutes or until almost tender. Remove foil.

Melt the butter in a saucepan. Add the rum, brown sugar, orange rind and stir well. Pour equal parts of the mixture into each pan reserving 1/3 of the mixture. Lift rings to allow liquid to run underneath. Bake uncovered for another 10 minutes. Turn the rings and pour the reserved rum mixture over them. Bake another 10 minutes.

Serve rings on a platter with pan juices poured over them.

Cannelloni with Spinach and Ricotta

2 1/2	tablespoons olive oil or melted butter
1	large onion, peeled and finely chopped
2	large cloves garlic, peeled and crushed
15	ounces can peeled tomatoes, chopped
1 1/4	tablespoons tomato paste
	salt and freshly ground black pepper
3/4	teaspoon dried basil
3/4	teaspoon dried oregano
3/4	pound cannelloni tubes
5	tablespoons thick spinach puree
1/2	pound ricotta cheese
2 1/2	tablespoons grated Parmesan cheese

To make the sauce: heat the oil and fry the onion and garlic for 2 to 3 minutes. Add the tomatoes and tomato paste and mix well. Simmer for 2 minutes. Add the salt and pepper, basil and oregano. Cover and simmer for 10 to 15 minutes until thick.

Cook the cannelloni tubes for 10 minutes in a large pot of salted water. Do not overcook. Lift out the cannelloni tubes and put them into a bowl of cold water to cool them quickly. Drain well. Mix together the spinach and ricotta. Add salt and pepper to taste. Fill the cannelloni tubes with the spinach mixture and arrange them in a greased shallow oven-proof dish. Pour the tomato sauce over the cannelloni and sprinkle with Parmesan cheese. Bake for 20 to 30 minutes at 350° or until the top is browned and bubbling. Serve immediately.

Zucchini Pie

1	cup zucchini, peeled and cubed
1/2	cup water
1	cup sugar
2	heaping tablespoons flour
1/2	tablespoon butter or margarine
1	egg
1	can Milnot
1	teaspoon vanilla
	unbaked pie crust
	nutmeg
	cinnamon

Put the zucchini in a half cup water and cook until thoroughly done. Drain well. Put zucchini in a blender, blend well and then add other ingredients. Pour into unbaked crust and sprinkle with nutmeg and cinnamon. Bake at 425° for 10 minutes, then 325°. Center of pie will not set while cooking, but will firm up when cold.

Note: Milnot is a canned milk replacement and can be obtained at larger supermarkets along with canned milk.

Sausage Zucchini Pie

4	cups thinly sliced zucchini
1	pound regular or mild Jimmy Dean sausage
1	cup chopped onion
1/4	cup margarine
2	tablespoons fresh parsley
1/2	teaspoon salt
1/2	teaspoon pepper
2	teaspoon French's mustard
4	teaspoons garlic powder
1/4	teaspoon basil
1/4	teaspoon oregano
2	eggs, beaten
8	ounces shredded mozzarella cheese
8	ounce tube Pillsbury crescent rolls

Unwrap the sausage and break it into pieces. Brown it lightly in a Dutch oven. Add onions, zucchini, margarine and cook for 10 minutes. Stir in the parsley and spices. Combine the beaten eggs and cheese. Stir into zucchini and sausage mixture.

Separate the crescent rolls into strips. Press over bottom and sides of an ungreased 7 1/2 by 11 3/4 inch baking dish. Sprinkle the crust with the mustard. Pour mixture into crust. Bake at 350° for 10 to 15 minutes or until the center is set. Let stand 10 minutes before serving.

Makes 4 to 8 servings.

Italian Vegetables

1	bunch broccoli, chopped
3	small zucchini, sliced
1	clove garlic, crushed
1	tablespoon olive oil
1	pound fresh mushrooms, sliced
1	pint cherry tomatoes, halved
1	teaspoon basil
1/2	teaspoon oregano
1	teaspoon salt
1/8	teaspoon crushed red pepper
1/8	teaspoon black pepper

Parboil broccoli and zucchini in the microwave for 5 to 7 minutes. In a large frying pan, sauté mushrooms and garlic in olive oil for 2 to 3 minutes. Add tomatoes, broccoli, zucchini and spices. Cover and cook about 3 to 5 minutes or until thoroughly heated. Stir occasionally. Enjoy. Great with steak or add 1 pound shrimp and serve on pasta.

Makes 8 servings.

Eggplant Parmesan

2	medium sized-eggplants
1/4	cup flour
	olive oil for frying
2	tablespoons olive oil
2	large cloves garlic, minced
6	tomatoes, peeled and coarsely chopped
1	stalk celery, minced
1	tablespoon fresh parsley, minced
2	carrots, minced
1	tablespoon fresh basil, chopped
1	large onion, minced
1/4	teaspoon salt
1/4	teaspoon sugar
1/4	teaspoon pepper
1/2	cup red wine
1/2	cup grated Parmesan cheese
1	pound Gruyere cheese, thinly sliced

Slice eggplant 1/2 inch thick, dip in flour, and fry in oil over high heat until soft.

Mix the next 11 ingredients and cook for 30 minutes. Add red wine and continue simmering until the sauce thickens.

Layer eggplant and sauce in a greased dish. Top with cheeses. Bake at 350° for 30 to 40 minutes.

Rueben Casserole

16	ounces sauerkraut, drained well
12	ounces sliced corn beef
8	ounces sliced Swiss cheese
1/2	cup mayonnaise
1/4	cup Thousand Island dressing
1	fresh tomato, sliced
4	slices rye bread, cubed
3	tablespoons melted margarine

Layer the first three ingredients. Mix the mayonnaise and the Thousand Island dressing, and spread it over the top. Cut the tomato over this.

Toss the melted margarine and bread together and put over the other ingredients. Bake in a 350° oven for 45 to 60 minutes.

Creamy Cheese Potatoes with Tony Packo's Sausage

2	pounds Idaho potatoes, sliced 1/8-inch thin
1	whole egg, beaten
1/2	cup grated Romano cheese
1 1/2	cups shredded Gruyere cheese
2	cups whipping cream
	white pepper to taste, salt if desired
1	pound Tony Packo Hot Dog Sausage links

Peel potatoes and rinse. Slice potatoes but do not rinse after slicing. Place potato slices in mixing bowl. Add egg and stir to coat slices. Spray casserole dish with non-stick coating. Layer potatoes, cheeses, white pepper and salt in the casserole dish. Place the last 10 slices vertically around the edge. Heat whipping cream to scalding and pour over potatoes. Bake covered for 1 hour. Add sausage links that have been scored every inch, about 1/3 of the way through. Bake 20 minutes more, uncovered.

Spicy Fried Cabbage

	half a head large, firm cabbage
4	tablespoons oil
1	large onion, sliced
2 to 3	green chilies, sliced
2	cloves garlic, crushed
1	teaspoon ginger, crushed
1	teaspoon tumeric
1 1/2	teaspoons salt

Shred cabbage. Heat the oil and fry the onion and chilies together, until soft. Add garlic and ginger. Fry, stirring until golden. Add tumeric and cabbage. Fry and toss on low heat for 15 minutes or until the cabbage is cooked and crunchy. Sprinkle with salt and mix. Serve as an accompaniment with rice.

Serves 6.

115

Marinated Brussel Sprouts

4	cups small brussel sprouts, cooked
1/2	cup tarragon vinegar
1/2	cup oil
1	small clove garlic, minced
1	teaspoon salt
	dash of hot pepper sauce
2	tablespoon sliced green onion

Place well-drained sprouts in glass bowl.

Mix all of the other ingredients and pour over sprouts. Cover and chill. Serve as hors d'oeuvres or as a salad with leafy lettuce greens.

Sauerkraut Salad

	about 2 cups, sauerkraut
1 1/3	cups bean sprouts, drained
2/3	cup celery, chopped
2/3	green and red peppers, diced
1/3	cup onion, chopped
3/4	teaspoon celery seed
3/4	cup suger
1/3	cup salad oil
1/3	cup vinegar

Mix first 6 ingredients thoroughly. Blend 3/4 cup sugar, 1/3 cup salad oil and 1/3 cup vinegar. Heat and stir until sugar is dissolved, then cool, and pour over salad mixture and let stand overnight in the refrigerator. Salad will keep several days under refrigeration.

Coleslaw to Freeze

1	medium head cabbage
1	large carrot, grated
1/2	green pepper, chopped
1	small onion, chopped

Dressing

1	cup vinegar
1/2	cup water
2	cups sugar
1	teaspoon celery seed
1	teaspoon mustard seed

For slaw: Add 1 teaspoon salt to cabbage, and let stand for 1 hour. Squeeze out juice, and add carrot, green pepper and onion.

For dressing: Combine ingredients and boil 1 minute. Cool until lukewarm. Pour over cabbage mixture and freeze.

Suggestion: Use a half head of red cabbage and a half head of green cabbage. This can be refrozen over and over. The recipe can be easily doubled and tripled.

Golden Potato Casserole

6	medium potatoes
1	pint sour cream
10	ounces sharp cheddar cheese, grated
1	bunch green onions
3	tablespoons milk
1	teaspoon salt
1/8	teaspoon pepper
2	tablespoons melted butter
1/3	cup bread crumbs

Cook scrubbed potatoes in salted water until just tender. Cool, pare and grate with a coarse grater. Do not use a food processor. Add sour cream, cheese, onion, milk, salt and pepper. Mix thoroughly. Turn into a buttered 9 by 13 inch pan, and smooth with a spatula. Combine the melted butter and bread crumbs, and sprinkle over the top. Bake in a 300° oven for 50 minutes or until piping hot. Cut in squares to serve.

Makes 8 servings.

Australian Stuffed Potatoes

1	pound bacon fried crisp and crumbled
2	cups sour cream
	baked potatoes

Slaw

8	cups white cabbage, shredded
4	cups red cabbage, shredded
4	cloves garlic, crushed
1	tablespoons tarragon, crushed

Dressing

2	teaspoons salt
2/3	cup sugar
1/2	cup cidar vinegar
2	cups mayonnaise
4	tablespoons heavy cream

Combine the slaw ingredients. Mix the dressing ingredients together and pour over the slaw. Mix and let stand for several hours before using.

Split potato and lightly butter. Top with slaw, then sour cream and bacon.

Tomato, Onion and Mushroom Flan

8	ounces basic pastry
2	cups grated cheddar cheese
4	tomatoes, skinned and chopped
1 1/4	tablespoons chives or parsley, chopped
1	cup mushrooms, sliced
2 1/2	teaspoons corn oil
1	large onion, peeled and chopped
3	eggs, beaten
1 2/3	cups milk
3/4	teaspoon salt
1/2	teaspoon freshly ground black pepper

Line a 8 to 9 inch flan dish with pastry. Put a quarter cup of the grated cheese into the pastry shell followed by the tomatoes, chives or parsley and the mushrooms. Heat the corn oil and fry the onion for 2 to 3 minutes. Mix the beaten eggs with milk, salt and pepper and fried onion. Pour into the flan shell and top with the remaining grated cheese. Bake at 400° for 35 to 40 minutes, or until set. Serve hot or cold.

Zucchini Pizza

6	ounces mozzarella cheese, grated
6	ounces cheddar cheese, grated
4	cups zucchini, grated
2	eggs, slightly beaten
2	tablespoons biscuit mix
1/4	teaspoon salt
2	tablespoons olive oil
1	large onion, minced
1	clove garlic, minced
1	pound ground chuck or round
1	cup tomato sauce
1	teaspoon oregano
	salt and pepper to taste

Combine 4 ounces of grated mozzarella cheese, 4 ounces of grated cheddar cheese, zucchini, beaten eggs, biscuit mix and 1/4 teaspoon salt. Press the mixture into a 10 by 15 inch jelly roll pan. Bake for 15 minutes in a oven preheated to 400°.

Sauté the onion, garlic and ground chuck or round in olive oil for 10 minutes and drain.

Add the tomato sauce and oregano to the meat mixture and add salt and pepper to taste.

Spoon the meat mixture onto the baked crust and top with 2 ounces of grated mozzarella and 2 ounces of grated cheddar.

Bake for 20 minutes in a 400° oven.

Zona's Four-way Bean Dish

1	can red kidney beans
1	can pinto beans
1	can French style green beans
1	can pork and beans
6	slices bacon
1	bunch green onions
1	green pepper chopped
3/4	cup brown sugar
1/2	bottle chili sauce

Mix and drain the 4 cans of beans. In a frying pan, brown the bacon, and sauté the onion and pepper. Add the brown sugar and chili sauce. Heat through. Pour mixture over beans and bake covered in a 325° oven for 1 hour.

Vegetable Pancakes

1	stick butter
2	cups carrots, shredded
2	cups zucchini, shredded
4	cups potatoes, shredded
1	medium onion, thinly sliced
3	eggs, beaten well
1	cup sour cream
5	tablespoons cornstarch
3/4	teaspoon salt
3/4	teaspoon freshly ground black pepper
	oil for frying
	lemon wedges

Melt the butter in a frying pan, and add the carrots, zucchini, potatoes and onion. Sauté for 3 to 4 minutes, stirring continuously. Beat the eggs together with the sour cream, cornstarch, salt and pepper. Mix well. Stir in the semi-cooked vegetables. Mix together gently. Heat a large non-stick frying pan and brush with 2 1/2 teaspoon oil, and add 1 1/4 tablespoon batter. Cook until light brown. Turn the small pancake over and cook until the other is also brown. Make 3 or 4 at a time. The size of the pancake can be increased by using more batter for each pancake.

Stuffed Summer Zucchini

2	large zucchini
1 1/2	cups fresh bread crumbs
1/2	teaspoon salt
1/4	teaspoon pepper
1/2	cup onion, chopped
4	small tomatoes, chopped
2	tablespoons butter, melted
1	cup sharp cheese, cubed
1/4	cup low-fat milk
6	slices cooked and crumbled turkey bacon

Preheat oven to 350°. Cut ends off zucchini and boil in salted water for 5 to 8 minutes. The zucchini is done when a knife pierces it without difficulty. Cut lengthwise and remove zucchini centers leaving the shell for stuffing. Chop the centers and set aside. Combine the remaining ingredients including the chopped zucchini centers. Fill the zucchini shells with mixture. Place in a baking pan. Bake at 350° for 25 minutes. This a beautiful and healthful summer dish that can be served hot or just warm.

Makes 4 to 6 servings.

Vegetable Sandwich

Sandwich

2	pounds cabbage, shredded
2	pounds carrots, shredded
1	cup green pepper, diced
1/2	teaspoon Tabasco sauce
1/2	teaspoon salt
1	cup mayonnaise
	toast with crusts removed

Cheese Spread

3/4	cup soft American cheese
1/2	teaspoon dry mustard
1/2	teaspoon Worcestershire sauce
1/2	teaspoon paprika
1/6	cup mayonnaise

Combine the sandwich ingredients, except the toast.

For cheese spread: Shred the cheese. When it reaches room temperature, combine it with the rest of the ingredients.

Makes 7 open-faced sandwiches.

Stuffed Eggplant

2	medium sized eggplants
	juice of half a lemon
1	medium onion, chopped
1/2	pound grated cheddar cheese
2	well-beaten eggs
1	cup dry bread crumbs
1/2	cup milk
	salt, pepper and dried basil to taste

Halve eggplants and parboil 15 minutes. Drain. Scoop out meat and mash. Reserve shells.

Mix remaining ingredients with mashed eggplant. Stuff shells. Bake at 350° until bubbly, about 30 minutes.

Scalloped Potatoes with Carrots and Onions

2	tablespoons flour
2	teaspoons salt
1/4	teaspoon pepper
3	medium sized potatoes, sliced
2	cups thinly sliced carrrots
1	large onion, thinly sliced
2	cups skim milk
1	tablespoon margarine
	paprika

Spray a 2-quart casserole with cooking spray. Combine flour, salt and pepper. Place alternating layers of potatoes, carrots and onions with a layer of flour mixture over each layer. Pour milk over all. Dot with butter and sprinkle with paprika. Bake 2 hours at 350°.

Baked Beans

1	16-ounce can butter beans
1	16-ounce can kidney beans
1	16-ounce can great northern beans
1	16-ounce can navy beans
3/4	cup brown sugar
1/2	cup molasses
1/2	cup ketchup
3	strips bacon, cut up
1	small onion, diced

Fry together the onion and bacon. Drain off some of the juice from the cans of beans. In a baking dish, mix the onion, bacon, beans, brown sugar, molasses and ketchup. Bake for 1 to 2 hours at 300°.

121

Broccoli Souffle

4	cups chopped broccoli
1	small clove garlic
2	tablespoons butter
2	tablespoons flour
1	cup milk or cream
1	tablespoon freshly grated Parmesan cheese
1/4	teaspoon salt
1/8	teaspoon white pepper
5	egg yolks
5	stiffly beaten egg whites

Parboil broccoli and garlic in water or chicken stock for 7 minutes. Drain and discard the garlic.

Melt the butter, add flour, and cook, stirring constantly for several minutes. Add milk or cream, Parmesan, salt and pepper. Stir until thickened.

Add a third of the sauce to the slightly beaten egg yolks. Then slowly add yolks to the remaining sauce, stirring constantly. Add broccoli.

Gently stir a third cup of the beaten egg whites into sauce, then fold in remaining whites. Pour ingredients into greased and floured souffle dish. Place dish in pan of hot water and bake at 350° for 30 to 40 minutes.

Roquefort Stuffed Tomatoes

8	medium tomatoes
8	tablespoons unsalted batter
1 1/4	pounds mushrooms, sliced
1	cup sour cream
2	tablespoons flour
4	ounces Roquefort cheese
1/4	teaspoon fine herbs
1/4	teaspoon basil
1/4	teaspoon lemon pepper
2	teaspoons parsley
2	tablespoons dry sherry
	salt and pepper to taste

Melt butter over moderate heat and sauté the mushrooms, stirring until all moisture is evaporated. In a bowl, stir the sour cream and flour, and add to mushrooms. Stir over low heat. Add remaining ingredients. Cool. Cut tomatoes in half, clean out seeds and stuff. Or cut the tops off tomatoes, clean out the seeds and stuff. Bake for 20 minutes at 375°.

Makes 8 servings.

Eggplant Casserole

2	medium eggplants
	oil
	salt
	pepper
	garlic salt
	dried parsley flakes
	eggs
	grated Parmesan cheese
	oil
	mozzarella cheese, sliced or shredded
	pasta sauce
	seasoned bread crumbs

With a potato peeler, strip the hard, outside skin of the eggplant. Slice the eggplant in 1/8-inch slices and place on paper towels. Sprinkle with salt, pepper, parsely and garlic salt. Let sit for 1 hour. (This is necessary to drain the liquid from the eggplant and avoid a watery, flat-tasting casserole.)

Dip each slice into beaten egg seasoned with salt, pepper, garlic salt, parsley and a sprinkle of Parmesan cheese. Then dip into bread crumbs and then egg again.

Fry each slice in oil. In a casserole dish, place layers of pasta sauce, eggplant, mozzarella cheese, pasta sauce and Parmesan cheese. Continue the layers in that order until the eggplant is all used.

Bake at 350° for 1 hour.

Zucchini Pie

3	medium zucchini, sliced
1	medium onion, chopped
1/2	cup vegetable oil
1	cup cracker crumbs
3	large eggs, beaten
1/2	teaspoon salt
1/2	teaspoon pepper
1/2	cup mozzarella cheese, grated
1/2	cup Parmesan cheese, grated
	butter
	parsley
	paprika
	green pepper rings

Cook zucchini and onion in oil until tender. Drain and mash with fork. Mix all ingredients except parsley, paprika and peppers.

Spoon into buttered pie pan. Sprinkle parsley and paprika over the top. Arrange peppers on top. Bake at 350° for 30 minutes. Cut into wedges.

Spinach Enchiladas

1	can cream chicken soup
8	ounces sour cream
10	ounces spinach
2	tablespoons minced onion
12	corn tortillas
4	cups shredded cheese
3/4	cup minced onion

Combine soup, sour cream, spinach and 2 tablespoons minced onion in the food processor. Fry the tortillas quickly, do not let them get crisp.

Put 1 tablespoon minced onion and 2 tablespoons cheese in each tortilla. Roll up and put in a greased 9x13 pan. Pour the spinach sauce over and top with the remaining cheese. Bake at 325° for 30 minutes.

Makes 6 servings.

Great for brunch or lunch.

Sauerkraut Balls

4	tablespoons butter
1	medium onion, ground
1	clove garlic, crushed
1/2	cup ham, ground
1/2	cup beef stock or broth
4	tablespoons flour, more if needed
3	cups sauerkraut, well drained and ground
1	tablespoon parsley, chopped fine

Melt butter in an iron skillet and add onion and garlic. Cook until transparent. Add ground ham and cook until very hot. Add the beef stock and cook until very hot. Add flour and cool over low heat until thick. Use more flour if necessary to stiffen. Be sure to squeeze the sauerkraut dry after grinding it, and then add sauerkraut and parsley. Refrigerate.

When cold, roll into balls, roll in flour, then dip in egg wash. Deep fry at 375°. They may be frozen if desired.

Summer Casserole

2	tablespoons margarine
1	medium onion, sliced thin
1/2	cup water
3	cups cut fresh or frozen green beans
3	cups summer squash, cut into 1 inch pieces
1/2	pound thinly sliced cooked type smoked sausage
10 1/2	ounce can condensed undiluted cream of mushroom soup
1/4	cup ketchup or tomato sauce

Cook onion in margarine until soft. Add water and beans. Cook covered for 10 minutes. Add squash and sausage. Cook covered for 5 minutes to crisp tender squash. Place in greased baking dish. Spoon mushroom soup on top and mix lightly. Drizzle with ketchup or tomato sauce, cover. Bake for 30 minutes at 350°.

Makes 6 servings.

Gratin Savoyard

1 1/2	pounds potatoes
2	cloves garlic
1	pint cream
4	tablespoons milk
	salt and pepper
	freshly grated nutmeg

Peel and thinly slice the potatoes. Spread on a table and sprinkle lavishly with salt. Rub slices together and heap them into a pile. Leave for ten minutes so salt can extract water, and soften the potatoes. Combine the cream, milk, a pinch of salt and grate a little nutmeg into the sauce pan. Set over high heat and bring to a boil for several minutes. Rub a medium gratin dish, preferably fine metal, with a half clove of garlic dipped in salt. Press the potatoes lightly between your hands to squeeze out water, and add the potatoes to the boiling cream and bring the mixture back up to a boil. Remove from heat and spread evenly in the prepared dish. The gratin should be 2 inches thick. Bake at 250° for 45 minutes.

Sauces & Accompaniments

Mint Pesto

1/2	cup pine nuts
6	cloves garlic
3	cups fresh mint
1	cup extra-virgin olive oil
	juice of 1 lemon
	crumbled chevre or feta cheese
	salt and freshly ground pepper to taste

Place the pine nuts and garlic in food processor and grind to paste. Add mint to food processor and again process into paste. While the food processor is running, add the olive oil in a thin steady stream. Add lemon juice and salt and pepper to taste. Process until blended. Serve with chevre or feta on dried toast or crackers.

Makes 1 1/2 cups.

Baked Barley

1/2	cup onion
6	tablespoons butter
1/2	cup barley
3	cups chicken broth
1/2	pound fresh mushrooms
1/2	cup slivered almonds

Sauté the onion in butter. Add the barley and brown lightly. Season. Pour into a casserole with 1 1/2 cups of the chicken broth. Cover. Bake at 350° for 30 minutes. Sauté mushrooms in butter. Add to casserole. Stir. Then add the other half of the chicken broth. Stir again and top with the slivered almonds. Bake 1 1/2 hours uncovered. It may be necessary to add some more broth. It can be held for a longer time by lowering the temperature and covering with foil.

Makes 6 servings.

Martinez Family Salsa

2 or 3	large fresh tomatoes
1	medium red onion
1	bunch green onions
1	bunch cilantro
2-4	fresh jalapenos, cooked
3	large cloves garlic
1	can stewed tomatoes
	salt
	garlic salt

Chop everything and let flavors mix overnight. Serve with tortilla chips or spoon over any Mexican dish.

Shrimp & Scallop Sauté with Lobster
Dill Sauce
by Chef Fifi Berry
Fifi's
1423 Bernath Parkway
South Village Square
Toledo, Ohio 43615
See Page 54

Fresh Tomato Sauce for Salmon

4 to 6	cups medium tomatoes
1	cup mayonnaise

Chop and drain tomatoes. Add pulp to mayonnaise. If desired, use juices to bring sauce to desired consistency. Excellent on grilled or broiled salmon.

Makes 4 to 6 servings.

Shrimp Sauce

1	cup ketchup
1/3	cup lemon juice
1	teaspoon Worcestershire sauce
20	drops Tabasco sauce
1	teaspoon salt
6	teaspoons horseradish.

Mix well and chill.

Elizabeth Barry's Mediterranean Couscous

Elizabeth Barry owns the Ginger Jar in Perrysburg, OH.

1	cup couscous
1 1/2	cups boiling water
1	teaspoon olive oil
2-3	green onions, chopped
3/4	teaspoon cumin
1/4	teaspoon turmeric
1/4	teaspoon cinnamon
1	cup drained, chopped canned plum tomatoes
3	tablespoons raisins
3	tablespoons pistachio nuts, or almonds, or pine nuts
3	tablespoons fresh parsley, chopped

Place couscous in baking dish. Add water and cover tightly with foil or plastic, allow to rest for 10 minutes, or until needed. Gently fluff with a fork.

Meanwhile, in a large skillet heat olive oil and add onion and cook gently for 3 minutes. Add cumin, turmeric and cinnamon and cook for 30 seconds. Add tomatoes, raisins, nuts and parsley and cook for a few minutes until thick.

Combine everything well, taste and adjust seasonings and serve with Ginger Jar Apricot and Green Ginger Chutney!

A delicious dish to serve with Summer Chicken. It looks like a grain, but it's pasta, made of semolina. Used to take a lot of cooking, steaming, drying, steaming, drying, but now it's instant!

Green Sauce

3	medium green tomatoes, coarsely chopped
4	tomatillos, chopped
1-2	jalapeno peppers, chopped
3	small garlic cloves, mashed
3	medium avocados
8	sprigs cilantro
1	teaspoon salt
1 1/2	cups sour cream

Bring tomatoes, tomatillos, peppers and garlic to a boil, let simmer 10-15 minutes. Cool. Mix with avocados, cilantro and salt in blender. Add sour cream.

Fresh Fruit Butter

1	cup (2 sticks) butter, softened
3/4	cup strawberries, raspberries or blueberries; or finely chopped apples, pears or dates; or grated peel of 1 lemon
	juice of 1 lemon

Cream butter, stir in fruit or peel and lemon juice. Refrigerate or freeze. These will keep up to 3 months in the freezer. Makes 1 1/2 cups.

The butter can be reshaped into butter sticks — wrapped, labeled, dated and frozen. Then when ready to use, cut off what you need and return remainder to freezer. Will keep up to one month in freezer. Remove butters from freezer or refrigerator several hours in advance of use so they will soften to spread.

Save small pimento jars, tiny mustard jars or baby food jars to store these butters. Browse in secondhand and antique shops, too, for odd, doll-sized cups and other little pots for packing butter. Spread the butter smoothly into containers, then top with foil or parchment cut to fit. Garnish with a sprig of parsley or appropriate piece of fruit and give a variety as gifts for neighbors.

Riverwalk, Findlay, Inspiration for
"By the Old Mill Stream"

Harvest, Ada

Fruit Dip

1	pint sour cream
4	tablespoons brown sugar
4	tablespoons Kahlua

Combine. Chill well and serve with any fruit.

Trout in Parsley Chive Sauce

4 to 6	small whole trout
1/4	pound butter
1/2	cup fresh parsley, chopped
1/2	cup fresh chives, chopped
1	pint heavy cream

Sauté trout in butter. When cooked properly, remove trout from pan, bone and keep warm. Add parsley and chives to pan juices and brown slightly while stirring. Add the cream. Stir and simmer until thickened. Spoon over trout fillets and serve.

Makes 4 to 6 servings.

Rhubarb Chutney

1	quart (4 cups) rhubarb, cut
1	pint (2 cups) onions, chopped
4	cups sugar
1	tablespoon salt
1	teaspoon allspice
1	teaspoon cayenne
1	teaspoon cinnamon

Mix all ingredients and boil until thick. This is an old family recipe.

Artichoke Dip

1	can artichokes, drained and chopped
1	4-ounce can chopped green chilies, drained
1	4-ounce can chopped pimentos, drained
1/2	cup grated Parmesan cheese
1 1/2	cups Hellmann's mayonnaise
1	8-ounce package hot pepper cheese, grated

Mix ingredients together. Bake in a shallow dish for 20 minutes at 350°. Serve with Doritos or corn chips.

Serves 10 to 12 people.

Vegetable Dip

1	cup mayonnaise
1	teaspoon onion salt
1	teaspoon onion flakes
1	teaspoon vinegar
1	teaspoon horseradish
1	teaspoon curry powder

Mix well. Chill, and serve with vegetables cut into bite-size pieces.

BBQ Sauce

1	gallon Open Pit Barbeque Sauce
2	cups Italian dressing
1	pound brown sugar
1	teaspoon dry mustard
2	tablespoons ginger

Mix well.

Brush generously on meat or fish.

Mexican Dip

1	pound ground beef (approx.)
1	package taco seasoning
1	can refried beans
1	cup extra-sharp cheddar cheese, grated

Brown beef in skillet and drain grease. Add the taco seasoning. Fill the empty taco package with water and add to beef. Let simmer for a couple of minutes. Mix in the refried beans. Put into ovenproof container. Top with grated cheese. Place in a 300° oven, or microwave, until the cheese is melted.

Elegant Rosemary Bean Spread

3	cups cooked or canned great northern white beans, rinsed and drained
1/3	cup rosemary flavored olive oil
1/2	teaspoon ground cumin
1	tablespoon dried cilantro
	kosher salt to taste

Whirl beans in a food processor. Add oil, cumin and cilantro. (If you are substituting cooking liquid for some of the oil, you may have to adjust the amounts to get a suitable texture.) Scrape bowl and process until fairly smooth. Taste and add salt. If you are planning to serve the spread on bread, make the mixture saltier than if you are planning to use on salted crackers.

Mound in a bowl. Cover and refrigerate to hold, but serve near room temperature for best flavor and texture.

135

Toledo Zoo Cafe
See Page 79

Scenic Maumee Bay State Park,
Oregon

Linguine with Mushrooms and Broccoli

3/4	cup ricotta cheese
1/2	cup Romano cheese, grated
3	teaspoons salt
1	brunch broccoli, trimmed and cut into small pieces
1	cup olive oil
4	cloves garlic, minced
1	pound mushrooms, sliced
1/2	teaspoon crushed red pepper
1	pound linguine

Combine the Romano and ricotta. Set aside. Bring a large stock pot of water to a rolling boil. Add a teaspoon salt and broccoli and cook for 7 minutes. Remove broccoli with slotted spoon. Save water to cook pasta.

Lightly brown garlic in a cup of olive oil, add mushrooms, and sauté for 7 minutes. Add salt, crushed red pepper, and stir in broccoli. Cook over low heat for 10 minutes. If mixture becomes too dry, add a few tablespoons of cooking liquid. Bring cooking liquid to boil, add more water if needed. Add linguine, stirring with a fork. Cook al dente for 10 to 15 minutes. Drain well. Stir into vegetable mixture. Toss with Romano and ricotta mixture. Serve in pasta bowls, and dust with additional Romano cheese.

Makes 8 servings.

Sweet Hot Fish Sauce and Caper Aioli

Sweet Hot Sauce

1	12-ounce jar red jalapeno jelly
2	tablespoons Chinese chili paste
5	tablespoons cider vinegar
1	tablespoon sugar

Caper Aioli

1	egg
3	cloves garlic, crushed
2	tablespoons capers, drained
2/3	cup olive oil
1	teaspoon salt
2	tablespoons boiling white vinegar

For sweet hot sauce: Heat ingredients together and then cool to room temperature.

For caper aioli: Add garlic, salt, capers and oil to egg. Using a stab blender, place on bottom of the container over egg. Mix oil, slowly raising blender. Add boiling vinegar and mix with blender.

Serve these two sauces with fish and chips.

Po' Boy Omelets

4	slices toast, white, wheat or rye
2	cups grated cheese, cheddar, monterey jack or mozzarella
1/2-1	cup milk
	butter
1	cup diced ham (optional)

Make 4 slices of toast. Butter on both sides. Place in the 9 inch square pan.

Sprinkle with 1 cup grated cheese. Beat 4 eggs and add 1/2 to 1 cup milk to cover bread. Pour over toast and sprinkle with the other cup of grated cheese. Put in a pre-heated 350° oven for 1 hour and the top is golden brown.

Serves 8.

Fettuccine in Cream Sauce

1	stick butter
1	pound fettuccine
1	cup heavy cream
1	egg
3/4	cups Parmesan cheese
1	teaspoon salt
1/4	teaspoon pepper

Combine butter and cream and warm until cream is room temperature. Add egg and mix well. Add cooked fettuccine, cheese, salt and pepper. Mix quickly and thoroughly over low heat. Serve immediately with more Parmesan cheese at the table.

Cheese Souffle

3	tablespoons butter
1	cup milk
1	slice white bread
1/2	teaspoon dry mustard
1	pinch nutmeg
1/2	teaspoon salt
1	cup shredded cheddar cheese, firmly packed
4	eggs, yolk and white separated

Preheat oven to 375°. In a sauce pan, heat the butter and add milk when melted. Allow steam, but do not scald. Tear the bread and put in a blender, adding dry mustard, salt and nutmeg. Cover blender and blend on high speed for 5 seconds. Add the hot butter-milk mixture and blend briefly. Add the shredded cheddar cheese and continue blending 10 seconds. Add the egg yolks and blend for an additional 10 seconds.

In a 1 1/2 quart souffle dish, beat the egg whites until stiff, but not dry. Gradually fold the cheese mixture into the beaten egg whites until lightly mixed. Bake for 35 minutes.

Makes 4 servings.

Sauder Farm & Village, Archbold

Red Barn, Delta

Rice Pilaf

2	tablespoons melted butter or margarine
1/2	cup onion, chopped
1	cup uncooked rice
2 1/2	cups water
2	chicken bouillon cubes
1/2	cup celery, diced
1/2	teaspoon rosemary

Melt butter in saucepan. Sauté onion for 5 minutes. Add rice and sauté until golden brown. Add remaining ingredients. Cover. Cook 15 minutes over low heat or until rice is tender.

Lucas County Library, Toledo
Classic Art Deco

Ned Skeldon Stadium, Home Of The
Mud Hens, Maumee

Breads

Apple Bread

2	cups all-purpose flour
1	cup sugar, divided
1	tablespoon baking powder
1/2	teaspoon salt
1	cup milk
1	egg
4	tablespoons (1/2 stick) butter, melted
1	Granny Smith apple, peeled, cored and diced
1/2	cup chopped walnuts
2	teaspoon ground cinnamon, divided
1	slice bread, made into crumbs

Preheat oven to 350°. Butter a 9 by 5 by 3 inch loaf pan. Combine the flour, a half cup of sugar, the baking powder and salt in a large bowl. Combine the milk, beaten egg and butter in a small bowl. Add to the flour mixture and stir until just moistened. Do not overmix.

Toss the apples with quarter cup of the sugar, the walnuts and 1 teaspoon of the cinnamon. Stir into the batter. Pour into the prepared pan. Combine the remaining quarter, 1 teaspoon cinnamon and the bread crumbs in a small bowl, and sprinkle over the top of the batter.

Bake for 1 hour or until a toothpick inserted into the center comes out clean. Cool the bread in the pan on a wire rack for 10 minutes. Loosen the edges and remove from the pan. Cool completely on a wire rack.

Raw Apple Bread

1/2	cup butter
1	cup sugar
2	eggs
2	cups flour
1/2	teaspoon salt
1/2	teaspoon baking soda
1	teaspoon baking powder
1	teaspoon cinnamon
1/2	teaspoon cloves
2	tablespoons buttermilk or soured milk
1-1 1/2	cups apples, unpeeled and coarsely chopped
1/2	cup coarsely chopped pecans or walnuts
1 1/2	teaspoons vanilla

Cream butter, add the sugar slowly and continue to beat until light. Beat in eggs. Sift flour and dry ingredients. Add to mixture, first half of flour mixture, then milk, then rest of flour. Stir in apples, nuts and vanilla.

Butter a loaf tin. Spoon batter into pan and bake in 350° oven for 45-60 minutes, or until straw or toothpick inserted into the loaf comes out clean.

Cool in pan about 5 minutes, then loosen from pan and turn out on rack. Makes 1 large loaf.

Special French Toast

1	stick margarine
1	teaspoon cinnamon
1	cup brown sugar
12	slices bread
1 1/2	cups milk
5	eggs

Melt the margarine and add the cinnamon and brown sugar. Mix. Put this mixture in the bottom of a 9 by 13 inch pan. Take the bread and double stack, placing 6 on the bottom and 6 on top. Flip each side of the double stacked slices over so that most of your melted mixture is now on the top slices. Mix the 1 1/2 cups milk with 5 eggs, and pour over the bread. Set overnight in refrigerator. In the morning, bake at 350° for 45 minutes.

Can be served with warm fruit and syrup.

Makes 6 servings.

Texas Hush Puppies

1	teaspoon sugar
1	teaspoon salt
1	cup flour
1	cup corn meal
1	cup chopped jalapenos
1/2	cup diced onions
1	tablespoon baking powder

Mix salt, sugar, flour and corn meal. Chop jalapenos very fine, and add to taste. If you are brave add two more. Onions should be diced very fine.

Add baking powder. Mix with buttermilk, add until pancake consistency. When grease is hot in the skillet, pour little pancakes, turn once, done when golden.

These are better than those hard ball puppies that so many people make.

Breakfast Muffins

4	eggs, beaten
1	cup oil
1	quart buttermilk
3	scant cups sugar
5	teaspoon baking soda
2	teaspoon salt
5	cups flour
6 1/4	cups raisin bran

Blend all ingredients in mixing bowl. Place in muffin tins. Bake at 375° for 20 minutes. Dough will hold in refrigerator for a few weeks.

147

World's Easiest Zucchini Bread

3	eggs beaten well
1	cup vegetable oil
2	cups sugar
2	cups grated, peeled zucchini
3	teaspoons vanilla extract
3	cup flour
1	teaspoon salt
1/4	teaspoon baking powder
1	teaspoon baking soda
3/4	teaspoon ground nutmeg
3	teaspoon ground cinnamon
1	cup chopped nuts

Mix together the first five ingredients. Sift together all other ingredients. Mix the wet ingredients with the dry ingredients. Grease and flour 2 loaf pans. Divide the batter evenly into each pan.

Bake at 350° for 1 hour, or until toothpick comes out clean when inserted into top of bread. Allow to cool on racks about a half an hour or until the top of the bread feels slightly cool to the touch. Invert and allow to cool completely. Store in zippered bags or tightly sealed plastic wrap.

Note: At the end of the summer when you have way too much zucchini left on the vines, you can easily peel, grate and freeze zucchini, if you put it in freezer bags. The bread itself gets a bit heavy when you freeze an already baked loaf, however.

Wort Bread

1	package dry yeast
1	tablespoon sugar
1/2	cup lukewarm water
1/2	cup milk, scalded and cooled
1/2	cup beer
1/2	cup molasses
1/4	cup shortening
3	tablespoons caraway seeds
	zest of 1 orange
1	tablespoon salt
1	egg, beaten
2	cups white, unbleached flour
1	cup rye flour
1	cup whole wheat flour
	additional white flour as needed

Proof the yeast in sugar and water. Add milk, egg and beer. Then start adding flours, intermixing with molasses, orange rind and seeds. When all ingredients are thoroughly mixed, knead for at least 5 minutes. Let rise until doubled, punch down and place in round pie plates. Let rise. Bake for 30 to 40 minutes at 350°.

Makes 2 small, round loaves.

A hearty and tasty bread.

Russian Tea Biscuits

Biscuits

2	cups flour
1/2	teaspoon salt
1/2	teaspoon baking powder
2/3	cup margarine (1 stick and 1 inch)
1	egg
1/2	cup orange juice

Filling

1	cup raisins
1	cup coarsely chopped walnuts
3/4	cup strawberry or raspberry jelly
1/2	teaspoon cinnamon

Combine the dry ingredients. Add margarine and mix with flour until crumbly, as with a pie shell. Add egg and orange juice and mix as a pie crust. Divide the dough in half. Roll out each half to a rectangle, approximately 6 by 10 inches. Combine filling ingredients and spread over dough. Roll up lengthwise and sprinkle with sugar. Cut into about 10 slices. Repeat for second half. Bake at 350° for 20 minutes.

Makes 20.

Apple Sauce Nut Bread

1	cup sugar
1	cup unsweetened apple sauce
2	cups all-purpose flour
1/4	cup vegetable oil
3	egg whites
3	tablespoons skim milk
1	teaspoon baking soda
1	tablespoon baking powder
1/2	teaspoon salt
1/2	teaspoon cinnamon
1/4	teaspoon nutmeg
1/2	cup nuts, chopped

Preheat the oven to 350°. Oil and flour a 9 by 5 by 3 inch loaf pan. Combine all the ingredients. Blend well. Fold in the nuts. Spread in the pan. Bake for 45 minutes or until it tests done. Cool in pan for 15 minutes, and then turn out to cool.

Makes 10 to 12 servings.

Coconut Bread

1/2	cup margarine
1	cup sugar
2	eggs
1 1/2	cups sifted flour
1	teaspoon baking powder
1/2	teaspoon salt
1/4	cup milk
1/4	cup cream of coconut
2	teaspoons coconut extract

Cream butter and sugar. Beat in eggs. Sift dry ingredients together and add to batter alternately with milk and cream of coconut. Add coconut extract. Pour into 9 by 5 by 3 inch pan. Bake at 325° for 1 hour.

Easy Banana Bread

1/2	cup (1 stick) butter or margarine
1	cup granulated sugar
2	eggs
1	cup mashed, ripe bananas
1 1/4	cups flour, plus one tablespoon
3/4	teaspoon baking soda
1/2	teaspoon salt (optional)
1/4	teaspoon cinnamon

Cream butter and sugar, add the eggs and beat until light. Add the mashed bananas and mix with electric beater until well mixed. Add the dry ingredients and mix on low until well blended.

Pour into a 5 by 9 inch bread pan greased with cooking spray or shortening.

Bake at 350° for 45 to 60 minutes, or until a toothpick comes out clean. Cool and wrap in foil.

Banana Raisin Pineapple Muffins

6	medium bananas
1	20-ounce can crushed pineapple, unsweetened
1	cup raisins
2	cups wheat flour
1/2	cup skim milk
1	tablespoon baking powder
1	tablespoon baking soda
1	tablespoon cinnamon
	Mazola no-stick corn oil spray

Mash the banana in a large mixing bowl. Add the remaining ingredients, and mix thoroughly. Spray muffin tins with Mazola no-stick corn oil spray. Bake at 400° for 35 to 45 minutes.

Makes 24 muffins.

Desserts

Zweiback

6	eggs
1	cup sugar
1 1/2	cups flour
1/2	cup chopped peanuts (unsalted)

Beat eggs about 3 minutes with an electric mixer. Add sugar and flour and beat 2 minutes. Stir in peanuts. Place in an oblong greased and floured pan. Bake at 350° for about 25 minutes. After it is cool, slice into narrow strips and place on a cookie sheet. Put in a warm oven and dry until lightly toasted.

Beulah Groves' Lady Baltimore Cake

See photo page 177

Cake

3/4	cup butter or other shortening
2	cups sugar
3	cups sifted cake flour
3	teaspoons baking powder
1/2	teaspoon salt
1/2	cup water
1/2	cup milk
1	teaspoon vanilla
6	egg whites (egg whites should be at room temperature to beat)

Icing and Filling

3	cups sugar
1	cup water
1/4	teaspoon cream of tartar
3	egg whites, stiffly beaten (should be at room temperature to beat)
1	teaspoon vanilla
1/2	cup chopped figs
1	cup chopped raisins
1	cup chopped pecans
	water to cover figs and raisins (bourbon may be added to the water for flavor)

For cake: Cream shortening and sugar together until fluffy. Sift flour, baking powder, and salt together 3 times. Combine water, milk and vanilla. Add small amounts of flour to creamed mixture, alternately with milk mixture, beating until smooth after each addition. Beat egg whites until stiff and fold into mixture. Pour into 3 9-inch greased pans. Bake in 350° oven for 30 minutes.

World's Best Carrot Cake

Cake

1 1/2	cups whole wheat flour
2/3	cup all-purpose flour
2	teaspoons baking soda
2	teaspoons cinnamon
1/2	teaspoon each ground ginger and ground nutmeg
1	cup granulated sugar
1	cup light brown sugar, firmly packed
1	cup buttermilk
3/4	cup vegetable oil
4	eggs
1 1/2	teaspoon vanilla
1	pound carrots, peeled and grated
1	8-ounce can drained, crushed pineapple
1	cup chopped walnuts
1	cup flaked coconut
1/2	cup golden raisins

Cream Cheese Frosting

1/2	cup butter, at room temperature
1	8-ounce package cream cheese, at room temperature
1	16-ounce box confectioners' sugar
2	teaspoon orange peel, grated
1	teaspoon vanilla

For cake: Preheat the oven to 350°. Sift together the flours, baking soda, cinnamon, salt, ginger and nutmeg onto a sheet of wax paper. Mix the sugar together in a large bowl. Stir in the buttermilk, vegetable oil, eggs (one at a time) and vanilla. Pour in the flour mixture, carrots, pineapple, nuts, coconut and raisins, stirring just until well blended.

Grease and flour three 9-inch round cake pans. Line the bottoms with wax paper; also, grease and flour the waxed paper. Pour the batter into the cake pans and bake for 30 minutes or until a tester inserted in the center comes out clean. Cool in pans for at least 10 minutes. Loosen the cake from the edges of the pans and invert onto wire racks. Peel off the waxed paper and cool completely.

For frosting: Beat butter and cream cheese together in a large mixing bowl until light. Add confectioners' sugar, orange peel and vanilla. Mix well.

Spread frosting between the layers and on top and sides of the cake. Cover and refrigerate overnight before cutting.

Cheesecake Royale

Crust

20	graham crackers
1/4	cup melted butter
2	tablespoons sugar

Filling

2	eggs
1/2	cup sugar
2	8-ounce packages Philadelphia cream cheese
1/2	teaspoon vanilla

Topping

3/4	pint sour cream, add more sugar if whole pint is used
2	tablespoons sugar, but 4 tablespoons is better
1/2	teaspoon vanilla

Have all ingredients at room temperature. Preheat the oven to 375°. Prepare the crust. Beat eggs thoroughly, adding sugar. Add the cheese and vanilla. Mix thoroughly. Place into crust to about 3/8 inch from top to allow for the topping. Bake for 20 minutes, and allow to cool completely. Then cover with topping and bake for 5 minutes only at 475°.

Elegant Chocolate Pie

Crust

2	cups finely chopped, toasted pecans
6	tablespoons brown sugar
6	tablespoons coarsely chopped butter
2 to 3	teaspoons dark rum

Chocolate Filling

1/2	pound butter
1 1/2	cups superfine sugar, confectioners sugar works best
2	squares unsweetened chocolate, melted
2	teaspoons vanilla
4	whole eggs
1/2	cup finely chopped pecans

For crust: Blend all ingredients for crust until the mixture holds together. Press into the bottom and sides of a 9 inch pie plate. Freeze for 1 hour.

For chocolate filling: Cream butter. Add sugar, and gradually blend in melted chocolate and vanilla. Add eggs one at a time. Beat 5 minutes after each egg. Stir in pecans. Pour mixture into the frozen pie crust. Let harden in the refrigerator, or it may be frozen. Garnish with whipped cream.

Makes 6 to 8 servings.

Popcorn Cake

6	quarts popped corn, with old maids removed
1	large package chocolate chips
1	stick butter (1/2 cup)
1	large package marshmallows
2	cups peanuts or mixed nuts
1	cup pecans (optional)

Melt chocolate chips, butter and marshmallows. Add nuts and mix. Pour over popped corn and mix. Place in buttered angel food pan and pack firmly. Let stand one hour before removing. Slice as you would any cake.

You may omit chocolate chips and add gum drops or soft candy. Caramel or butterscotch chips are also good. Cracker Jack or Caramel Corn can be used.

Heavenly Chocolate Dessert

1	small angel food cake, baked
2	packages instant chocolate pudding
3	cups milk
2	packages whipped cream topping
6	Heath bars

Tear angel food cake into pieces and place in a 9 or 10 inch square pan. Mix instant chocolate pudding with 2 cups milk, pudding will be thick. Whip topping with 1 cup milk. Blend pudding and the topping together. Pour over the angel food cake pieces. Mix slightly. Cover and chill until serving time. Crush Heath bars and just before serving, sprinkle over the top. Note: This can also be mixed together and served in parfait glasses.

Makes 8 to 10 servings.

Death by Chocolate

1	baked chocolate cake
1/2	cup Kahlua liqueur
	large box prepared instant chocolate pudding
1	pint whipping cream
6	crushed Skor candy bars
	large parfait dish or casserole dish

Poke holes in the chocolate cake prior to removal from baking pan. Drizzle Kahlua over cake. Crumble cake. In a large dish, layer chocolate cake, pudding, Skor bars and whipped cream. Repeat layers, ending with a layer of whipped cream. Refrigerate 2 to 4 hours for best result. Serve in hot weather for really smiley faces.

Makes 8 servings.

155

Graham Cracker Fluff

2	egg yolks
1/2	cup sugar
3/4	cup milk
1	package Knox unflavored gelatin
1/2	cup cold water
2	stiffly beaten egg whites
1	teaspoon vanilla
1	cup whipping cream
12	graham crackers (crushed)
3	tablespoons melted butter
3	tablespoons sugar

Beat egg yolks, add sugar and milk. Cook in double boiler until slightly thickened. Soak gelatin in cup cold water. Pour hot mixture over softened gelatin and stir until smooth. Chill until slightly thickened. Add egg whites, vanilla and whipping cream to chilled mixture.

Combine graham crackers, melted butter and sugar.

Mix until crumbly. Spread half of the crumbs in the bottom of serving dish. Add pudding mixture and sprinkle remaining crumbs over the top. Chill in refrigerator until set. May be used as a dessert or salad.

Lime-Orange Deluxe

This recipe appeared in the Palladium Item, Richmond, Indiana in May 1953.

1	cup bottled milk, scalded or 1/2 cup evaporated milk with 1/2 cup water, scalded
2	eggs, slightly beaten
1/4	cup granulated sugar
1/8	teaspoon salt
1	tablespoon plain, unflavored gelatin
1	cup orange juice
1/4	cup lime juice
3/4	cup corn syrup
1	cup cream, light or heavy
1 1/2	teaspoons grated orange rind
1 1/2	teaspoons grated lemon rind
	crushed ice
	ice cream salt
	raspberries, optional

Slowly stir milk, eggs, sugar and salt together. Cook over hot, not boiling water and stir until mixture coats the spoon, about 5-6 minutes.

Soak gelatin in orange juice for 5 minutes. Stir into the custard the lime juice and corn syrup. Cool. Add cream.

Freeze in 2-quart crank or electric freezer until it is difficult to turn, using 8 parts of crushed ice and 1 part ice cream salt.

When almost frozen, add orange and lemon rind and finish freezing. Serve topped with raspberries.

Raspberry Pie

whipped cream

Crust

3/4	cup crushed pecans
1	stick margarine
1	cup flour

Filling

1 1/2	cup sugar
1/4	cup cornstarch
1 1/2	cups water
1	3-ounce package raspberry gelatin
1	quart raspberries

For a 9 inch pie shell, bake the crust ingredients for 20 minutes. Cool. Cook the filling ingredients until clear. Add gelatin and then raspberries. Decorate with whipped topping. Refrigerate.

Makes 8 servings.

Ma Heiber's Famous "Healthy" Banana Cake

2/3	cup margarine
1 1/2	cups sugar
1/2	cup brown sugar (optional)
2	eggs
1	cup mashed, very ripe bananas
1	tablespoon sour cream
1 1/2	cups flour
1/4	cup wheat germ
1/4	cup oat bran or 2 cups of flour can be substituted for above 3 ingredients
1	teaspoon baking soda
1	12-ounce bag chocolate chips
	handful golden raisins (optional)
1/2	cup chopped nuts (optional)
	powdered sugar (optional)

Bananas that have gotten very ripe and then were frozen can be used for this recipe. They are excellent for this cake. Don't bother to measure the bananas. Depending on their size, it may take 3, 4 or 5 bananas.

Cream the shortening. Add sugar(s) and unbeaten eggs and mix well. Add bananas and dry ingredients and sour cream. Add chocolate chips, raisins and nuts last.

Bake at 350° in a greased, floured 9 by 13 inch pan for about 35 minutes. Do not overbake. If cake is moist, it is very good. Powdered sugar may be sprinkled on top when cool.

Makes a lot.

Peach Kuchen

2	cups sifted all-purpose flour
1/4	teaspoon baking powder
1/2	teaspoon salt
1	cup sugar
1	stick butter
12	peach halves (fresh, frozen or canned)
1	teaspoon cinnamon
1	cup heavy cream
2	egg yolks

Sift the flour, baking powder, salt and 2 tablespoons of the sugar together. If you have a food processor, mix the flour mixture with the butter until it looks like small peas, or simply use a pastry blender. Pat an even layer over the bottom and half way up the sides of a 9 inch square baking pan. Place peach halves, peeled and drained, over the pastry. Sprinkle mixture of cinnamon and the rest of the sugar over the peaches and bake in a preheated oven at 400° for 15 minutes. Now mix 2 egg yolks and cream together and pour over the peaches. Bake 30 minutes longer. Serve warm.

Prepare everything early in the day and bake it while your guests are eating. This is an easy dish that reaps big rewards.

Pumpkin Pie Cake

Crust

1	box yellow cake mix (reserve one cup)
1	beaten egg
1	stick margarine, softened

Filling

1	29-ounce can pumpkin
3	eggs, beaten
2	teaspoons cinnamon
1	small can or 2/3 cup evaporated milk
1	cup sugar

Topping

1	cup cake mix
1/2	cup sugar
1/4	cup margarine, melted
1	cup nuts

For crust: Mix ingredients, less 1 cup of the cake mix and press into a 9 by 13 inch pan.

For filling: Mix filling and spread over crust.

For topping: Mix until it crumbles. Spread on top of the filling. Bake 1 hour and 15 minutes at 350°.

Makes 24 servings.

Praline Crunch

1	16-ounce box Quaker Oat Squares
2	cup pecans or walnuts, cashews can be mixed in
1/2	cup brown sugar
1/4	cup margarine
1/2	cup corn syrup, Karo
1	teaspoon vanilla
1/2	teaspoon baking soda

Mix cereal and nuts and set aside. Microwave the corn syrup and margarine for 1 1/2 minutes on high. Stir. Microwave for 30 seconds to 1 1/2 minutes or until boiling. Add the vanilla and baking soda. Stir into hot mixture. Pour liquid over cereal mix and blend well. Bake mix at 250° for 1 hour. Stir every 15 minutes. Pour onto wax paper. Allow to cool until it is not sticky. Serve.

Makes 10 cups.

Cheese Pie Dessert

1	package lemon gelatin
1	cup boiling water
1	8-ounce package Philadelphia cream cheese
1	cup sugar
1	large can Pet milk (refrigerate ahead of time, it must be very cold)
	juice of 2 lemons
1/2	teaspoon vanilla

Dissolve gelatin in boiling water. Refrigerate until partially congealed. Add cream cheese, sugar, vanilla and lemon juice to the partially congealed gelatin. Beat until smooth and fluffy. Beat milk in a large cold bowl until very stiff and peaks form, fold in cheese mixture. Pour into baked graham cracker crust, makes 2-9 inch pies or 1-9 by 12 by 2 inch pan. Refrigerate until set.

Makes 12 servings.

Caramels

1/4	pound margarine, not low fat
1 1/2	pounds white sugar
1 3/4	pounds corn syrup
1	large can Carnation milk
2	teaspoons vanilla
1	cup walnuts or pecans (optional)
	chocolate

Melt the margarine in a large pan. Add the sugar, the corn syrup and the Carnation milk. Cook over moderate heat to 240°, stirring constantly. Remove from heat. Stir in 2 tablespoons of vanilla. Add nuts if desired. Pour into very generously buttered 9 by 13 inch pan. Cool completely. Remove candy from pan onto wax paper. Cut into squares, and hand dip in chocolate or wrap in wax paper.

Makes about 5 pounds of candy when dipped in chocolate.

Snickerdoodles

3 1/2	cups all-purpose flour
1/2	teaspoon cream of tartar
1/2	teaspoon baking soda
1/2	teaspoon salt
1	cup butter or margarine
2	cups sugar
2	eggs
1/4	cup milk
1	teaspoon vanilla
3	tablespoons sugar
1	teaspoon ground cinnamon

Grease a cookie sheet. Stir together flour, soda, cream of tartar and salt. Beat butter for 30 seconds. Add the 2 cups sugar and beat until fluffy. Add eggs, milk and vanilla. Beat well. Add dry ingredients and beat until well combined. Form dough into 1-inch balls, roll in mixture of remaining sugar and the cinnamon. Place balls 2 inches apart on cookie sheet and flatten slightly with the bottom of a drinking glass. Bake at 375° about 8 minutes or until golden brown.

Walnut Yogurt Ring

Cake

1	cup walnuts
1	cup sugar
2/3	cup butter
2	eggs
8	ounces plain yogurt
1	teaspoon vanilla
2	cups sifted flour
1 1/2	teaspoons baking powder
1/2	teaspoon baking soda
1/4	teaspoon salt
1/2	teaspoon cinnamon
	9 inch tube pan

Powdered Sugar Glaze

1	cup powdered sugar
1 1/2	tablespoons warm water
	A few drops vanilla

Chop the walnuts coarsely. Cream butter with three-quarters cup sugar until light and fluffly. Beat in eggs one at a time until well blended. Stir in the yogurt and vanilla. Resift flour with baking powder, baking soda and salt. Add to creamed mixture until smooth. Add only three-quarters cup walnuts. Turn half the mixture into greased and floured 9 inch tube pan. Mix the remaining batter and sprinkle with remaining quarter cup walnuts. Bake below oven center at 350° for about 1 hour or until the cake tests done. Cool 10 minutes, then remove outside rim of cake pan.

To make the powdered sugar glaze, combine 1 cup sifted powdered sugar with the warm water. Add a few drops of vanilla. Drizzle with powdered sugar glaze while warm.

Serve with fresh strawberries, raspberries, orange slices, pineapple chunks, etc.

Zebra Cake

Cake

3/4	cup all-purpose flour
1/4	cup cocoa
1	teaspoon baking powder
1/4	teaspoon salt
3	eggs
1	cup sugar
1/3	cup water
1	teaspoon vanilla
1/4	cup (approximately) chopped hazelnuts

Cream Filling

1	cup ricotta cheese
1/3	cup light cream or half & half
3/4	cup butter or margarine, softened
1	cup powdered sugar
2	teaspoons vanilla
1	cup hazelnuts, grounded or finely chopped

Chocolate Glaze

1	one-ounce square unsweetened chocolate
1 1/2	tablespoons butter or margarine
1/2	cup powdered sugar
1/2	teaspoon vanilla
1	tablespoon hot water

For cake: Heat oven to 375°. Line a 15 1/2 by 10 1/2 by 1 inch jelly roll pan with aluminum foil or waxed paper; grease (do not use spray). Mix flour, cocoa, baking powder and salt. Set aside. Beat eggs in small mixing bowl for about 5 minutes or until the mixture is very thick and lemon-colored. Pour eggs into a large mixing bowl and gradually beat in sugar. Mix in water and vanilla on low speed. Add cocoa mixture gradually, beating just until batter is smooth. Pour into pan, spreading batter to corners. Bake for about 13 to 14 minutes or until a wooden pick inserted into center comes out clean. Remove from pan. Cool.

For cream filling: Measure cheese and cream into blender. Cover. Blend until smooth. Set aside. Beat batter until light. Gradually add sugar, beating until light and fluffy. Beat in cheese mixture and vanilla gradually. Filling may appear curdled. Stir in ground hazelnuts. Refrigerate.

For chocolate glaze: Melt chocolate and butter over low heat. Remove from heat. Mix in sugar and vanilla. Stir in water, one teaspoon at a time, until glaze reaches proper spreading consistency.

Cut cake crosswise into 4 equal parts. Spread about one cup of cream filling on each of three layers. Stack layers, with a plain layer on top. Frost top with chocolate glaze. Sprinkle with chopped hazelnuts. Refrigerate until serving time, but no longer than 36 hours.

Makes 8 to 12 servings.

Baked Pineapple Delight

1/2	cup sugar
2	teaspoon flour
3	eggs
1	large can crushed pineapple
2	slices bread
1	stick butter or margarine

Mix the sugar and flour. Beat the eggs well and mix with the sugar and flour. Add the crushed pineapple. Mix. Put in greased baking dish and crumble the bread on top. Slice stick of butter on top. Bake for 1 hour at 400°. Put over baked ham.

Serves 6.

Apples with Crispy Top

4 to 6	medium apples
3/4	cup quick cooking oatmeal
1/2-3/4	cup brown sugar
1/2	cup flour
1/2	cup butter or margarine

Arrange apples slices in 8 or 9 inch round pan. Combine oatmeal, sugar and flour. Cut in butter until crumbly. Sprinkle this mixture over apples and bake at 350° for 35 to 40 minutes. Serve warm.

Makes 6 to 8 servings.

Cream Pie Filling

	baked pie shell
Filling	
2 1/2	cup milk, save 1/2 cup
1/2	cup sugar
3	tablespoon cornstarch
1/4	teaspoon salt
3	eggs
1	teaspoon vanilla
Meringue	
3	egg whites
	dash salt
1/4	teaspoon cream of tartar
6	scant tablespoons sugar

For meringue: Beat the eggs with a dash of salt and the cream of tartar. Just before stiff, add the sugar. Then finish beating until stiff. Be sure to beat long enough for sugar to dissolve.

For filling: Heat 2 cups of milk in a pan, but do not boil. In a bowl, mix sugar, cornstarch, salt and egg yolks with the half cup milk. Mix until smooth and pour into hot milk, stirring all the time. Cook over low heat until thick, like pudding. Cool until lukewarm, and add vanilla. Put into baked pie shell, top with meringue and brown.

This cream filling is good as is, or may be used with bananas, coconut, pineapple, etc.

Onesie Brunchcakes

1	cup all-purpose flour
1	tablespoon baking powder
1/4	teaspoon salt
1	tablespoon brown sugar
1	cup milk
1	egg
1	tablespoon butter, melted
1	cup fresh blueberries or dried peaches

Sift flour, baking powder, salt and sugar together. Beat egg in milk and add melted butter. Stir ingredients together. Leave lumpy. Add fruit. Drop by spoon onto a lightly greased skillet. Turn once when bubbles start to appear.

Makes 3 to 4 servings.

Todd Biggs of Creative Gourmet's Ginger-Orange Strawberry Shortcake

Tender shortcakes accented with fresh, candied ginger are a delicious complement to the strawberry filling.

Shortcakes

2	cups all purpose flour
2	tablespoons finely chopped, crystallized ginger
4	teaspoons finely chopped, peeled, fresh ginger
1	tablespoon baking powder
1	tablespoon sugar
1	teaspoon grated orange peel
1/2	teaspoon salt
1/4	cup (1/2 stick) chilled, unsalted butter, cut into pieces
3/4	cup chilled whipping cream
1	egg, beaten to blend (glaze)

Filling

3	1-pint baskets strawberries, hulled, thickly sliced
10	tablespoons sugar
2	cups chilled whipping cream
1	teaspoon vanilla extract
	powdered sugar

For shortcakes: Mix flour, both gingers, baking powder, sugar, orange peel and salt in a bowl. Rub in butter until mixture resembles coarse meal. Add cream; stir with fork until clumps form. Gather dough into ball. Wrap in plastic, chill 1 hour.

Preheat oven to 350°. Line a large baking sheet with parchment. Roll out the dough on a floured surface to 1/4-inch thickness. Using floured, 3-inch diameter cookie cutter, cut out rounds. Place on baking sheet. Reroll scraps, cut out additional rounds for 6 rounds total. Brush with glaze. Bake until shortcakes are golden, about 30 minutes. Transfer to rack and cool.

For filling: Combine strawberries and 6 tablespoons sugar in large bowl. Transfer half of berry mixture to another bowl. Using fork, crush strawberries in 1 bowl to chunky sauce consistency. Let both bowls stand at room temperature until juices form, about 20 minutes.

Beat cream, vanilla and remaining sugar in a bowl until soft peaks form. Cut shortcakes in half. Place 1 bottom half in each of 6 bowls. Spoon some crushed berries over each, then top with generous amounts of sliced berries. Spoon whipped cream over. Cover with shortcake tops. Dust with powdered sugar.

163

Mother's Date Pudding

1	cup dates
1	cup walnuts
1	cup graham crackers
1	cup marshmallows
	evaporated milk

Grind dates, nuts, graham crackers and marshmallows. Add just enough evaporated milk to hold the mixture together. Form into a log and roll in additional graham cracker crumbs. Refrigerate.

Slice and serve with a dollop of whipped cream.

Pice Ary Maen (South Wales Cakes)

1/2	cup margarine
1/2	cup sugar
1	egg
2	cups unbleached flour
1/4	teaspoon salt
1	teaspoon baking powder
1/4	teaspoon mace
1/2	cup currants

Cream margarine and sugar. Add egg, and mix well. Gradually add the sifted dry ingredients. Add currants last. Roll on floured surface, and cut with cookie cutter a half inch thick. "Bake" on top of the stove with medium heat in an iron skillet or an electric fry pan set at 325° for 5 to 8 minutes on each side or until brown. Watch carefully.

The texture is "sandy," but these are good warm or cold.

Makes 16 cakes.

Delicious Rice Pudding

2	cups hot cooked rice, cooked in 1/8 teaspoon salt
1 1/2	cup sugar
1	teaspoon vanilla
4	eggs, separated
1/2	cup butter or margarine
2	cups half & half or coffee cream
2	cups milk
	raisins to taste

Mix sugar and butter in hot rice. Beat egg yolks and pour over hot rice. Mix half & half, milk, vanilla and pour into rice mixture. Beat egg whites till peaked and fold into rice mixture. Add raisins to taste.

Place in a greased baking dish and set dish in pan of hot water. Bake at 350°. When a knife inserted in the center of the rice pudding comes out clean, it is done.

Joe Crea's Honeyed Peach and Pecan Upside-Down Cake

Cook's notes: Before measuring honey, syrups or other liquid sweeteners, first lightly coat, inside of measuring cup with a non-stick cooking spray. You will bake the cake in the same pan in which you've melted the topping and added the fruit; a straight-sided 10-inch Dutch oven or a deep cast-iron skillet is perfect. (The iron pan may darken the topping slightly; it's best not to store the cake in an iron pan.) Coat surface of the sides of the pan with non-stick spray before spooning in the batter. If you prefer, drained pineapple segments can be used in place of the peach halves.

Topping

1/2	cup (1/2 stick) unsalted butter
1	cup (packed) light brown sugar
1/2	cup light honey, such as orange blossom (see cook's notes)
1	can (29-ounce) cling peach halves, drained (see cook's notes)
1	heaping cup pecan halves or pieces
10-12	maraschino cherries, drained and patted dry

Cake

1	cup (2 sticks) unsalted butter, at room temperature
1 1/3	cups all-purpose flour
5	eggs, at room temperature
1 1/3	cups sugar
1 1/2	teaspoons baking powder
1/2	teaspoon salt
1/2	teaspoon almond extract
1/2	teaspoon vanilla extract

For the topping, melt the butter in a straight-sided 10-inch Dutch oven (or a deep, 10-inch cast-iron skillet) with heat-proof handles. Add the brown sugar and cook, stirring often, just until mixture starts to bubble. Stir in the honey. Remove pan from heat and place on a cake rack. Allow the cake to cool to room temperature. When cool, stir the syrup mixture before adding the fruit. Place a cherry in the hollow of each peach half. There should be at about 10 halves. Arrange decorated peaches on top of the stirred syrup, hollow-side-down. Scatter pecan pieces among the fruit. Set aside while preparing the cake batter.

To make the batter, place butter and flour in a large bowl. Beat with an electric mixer on low speed, until mixture is like meal and well-blended, or for about 6 minutes. Add eggs one at a time, beating on low speed or by hand with a wooden spoon.

Sift together the sugar, baking powder and salt. Add almond and vanilla extracts and the dry ingredients to the butter mixture, mixing at low speed with an electric mixer or by hand until combined. The batter will be heavy.

To assemble the cake and bake, carefully spoon batter onto the fruit and nuts. Bake in a 325° oven for 45 minutes to 1 hour, or until a cake tester inserted in center comes out clean. Loosely cover cake with a piece of foil if the top begins to brown too quickly towards the end of baking time.

Remove the cake from the oven to a wire rack and cool to room temperature. The cake may be stored at room temperature in a pan for 24 hours, but it is necessary to place pan over low heat to slightly warm the syrup for easier unmolding.

To present the cake, when it is cool, run a thin, metal spatula around the edge to loosen from the pan. Place a serving plate on top of the pan and invert the cake. Serve at room temperature, either plain or with a dollop of unsweetened whipping cream.

Makes 8 to 12 servings.

Pennsylvania Dutch Brown Pudding

1 1/2	cups brown sugar
2	cups water
3	tablespoons butter
1	cup flour
1/2	cup milk
3	tablespoons baking powder
1/2	teaspoon salt
1	teaspoon cinnamon
1/2	teaspoon vanilla
1/2	cup walnuts (optional)
1/4	cup raisins (optional)

Combine 1 cup brown sugar, water and butter in a saucepan. Bring to a boil. Boil for 1 minute. Pour into an 8 by 8 inch pan.

Mix 1/2 cup brown sugar, flour, milk, baking powder, salt, cinnamon, and vanilla and walnuts and raisins if desired. Drop by spoonfuls onto hot brown sugar mixture. Bake at 350° for 25 minutes or until top is brown.

Makes 6 servings.

This recipe goes back to the Pennsylvania Dutch Community near Connellsville, Pennsylvania, around the turn of the century.

Mike's Death by Chocolate

1	19.8 ounce family size brownie mix
3	3 1/2 ounce boxes chocolate mousse or enough mousse to mix to make 6 cups
8	Heath bars (crushed)
2	12 ounce container cool whip
1/4-1/2	cup Kahlua or coffee

Bake brownies according to directions on box and allow to cool. Using a fork, punch holes in the cooled brownies. Take your Kahlua (coffee) and drizzle over the brownie and set aside. Make up chocolate mousse according to the directions. Crush Heath bars either with a food processor or by tapping with a hammer. This is a layered dessert and looks best when served in a trifle bowl. First layer half your brownies in the bottom of the bowl then cover with one half of the chocolate mousse. Sprinkle one half of the heath bars over the mousse, and then take 1/2 of the cool whip and place on top. Now repeat the above to complete the dessert. Using the back of a teaspoon you can put peaks in the cool whip. Keep this dessert refrigerated till ready to serve.

Makes 20 servings.

Variations

Instead of the Kahlua, you may substitute a mixture of 1 teaspoon of sugar with 4 tablespoons of leftover black coffee. During the holiday season, you may want to tint your cool whip with food coloring. Also, for a more unique dessert, you might want to flavor your cool whip with: mint, amaretto or almond extract.

Willa's Sour Cream Apple Pie

	pastry for a single crust pie
4 to 5	apples, peeled, cored and sliced
6	tablespoons flour
6	tablespoons sugar
1/3	cup sugar
1/2	cup sour cream

Put the apples into a medium sized bowl and stir in flour and sugar. Pour into a prepared crust. Pour sugar and sour cream over the apples, and sprinkle with cinnamon. Bake 15 minutes at 400° and then an additional 30 minutes at 325°.

Peanut Butter Chip Pie

1	unbaked pie crust
1/2	cup butter, melted
1	cup peanut butter chips
1	cup sugar
2	eggs
1/2	cup flour
1	teaspoon vanilla
1	cup pecan halves

Melt butter and chips together. Beat eggs, sugar, and vanilla together. Add chip and butter mixture. Slowly add flour, mixing well. Pour into unbaked pie shell. Cover top of pie with pecan halves and bake 30 minutes at 350°.

Funnel Cake

3	eggs
2 1/4	cups milk
3	cups flour
3/4	teaspoon salt
1 1/2	teaspoon baking powder
	powdered sugar

Beat eggs and add milk. Combine flour, salt and baking powder and sift into liquid ingredients. Deep fry into hot oil, drain and dust with powdered sugar.

The trick to making funnel cakes is in drizzling the batter into the hot oil. Fill a funnel with batter (put your finger over the end!), hold it over the oil and drizzle the batter in circles, starting in the center of the pan and working outward in larger circles. As you make larger circles, criss-cross with batter to connect the circles to make a solid cake. When golden brown on bottom, turn over and brown the other side.

167

Marcy Kaptur's Capitol Hill Coffeecake

1/4	cup butter flavored Crisco
1 1/4	cups sugar
1	egg
1/2	cup milk
2	cups flour
2	teaspoons baking powder
1/2	teaspoon salt
2	cup blueberries (fresh, drained)

Topping:

1/2	cup sugar
1/3	cup flour
1	teaspoon cinnamon
1/4	cup margarine

Cream together the Crisco and 3/4 cup sugar, and add the egg, a 1/2 cup milk and 2 cups of flour. Mix until supple but not runny or stiff. Add more milk if necessary.

Add 2 teaspoons of baking powder, 1/2 teaspoon for salt and 2 cups of blueberries.

For the topping, mix ingredients and sprinkle on top. Bake at 350° for 30-40 minutes.

Gram's Best Cookies

1	cup brown sugar
1	cup sugar
1	cup butter
1	egg
1	cup salad oil
1	cup crushed corn flakes
1	cup regular rolled oats
1/2	cup shredded coconut
3/4	cup chopped walnuts or pecans
3 1/2	cups all-purpose flour
1	teaspoon baking soda
1/2	teaspoon salt
1	teaspoon vanilla extract

Preheat an oven to 325°. Cream together the sugars and butter until fluffy. Add egg. Mix well. Add salad oil, and again mix well. Add corn flakes, oats, coconut and nuts. Stir well. Add flour, soda, salt and vanilla.

Mix well. Form dough into balls about the size of walnuts, and place on an ungreased cookie sheet. Flatten the cookies with a fork, dipping the fork in water. Bake for 12 minutes.

Makes 8 dozen.

A Pot of Dirt

2	cups milk
1	package worms (gummi style)
1	new, well scrubbed 8-9 inch flower pot
1	stick (1/2 cup) butter
1-1 1/2	packages Double Stuff Oreo cookies, crumbled to resemble dirt
1	8-ounce package cream cheese
8	ounces whipped topping
1	small package instant vanilla or chocolate pudding
1/2	cup powdered sugar

In a large bowl mix cream cheese, whipped topping, butter, powdered sugar, pudding mix and milk. Fold in all of the worms, except four. Layer cookie crumbs with above mixture into clean flower pot. End with crumbs on top. Arrange four worms so they are partially hidden by "topsoil".

Chill. Serve with artificial or silk flowers stuck in pot and a <u>clean</u> trowel or small garden shovel for serving.

Chocolate Mousse Cake

Genoise

4	eggs
1/2	cup sugar
1/2	cup flour
2	ounces melted unsalted butter

Syrup

3 1/2	ounces sugar
3 1/2	ounces water
3 1/2	ounces rum

Mousse

8	egg yolks
3	tablespoons cocoa powder
1	pound 2 ounces softened unsalted butter
9	ounces baking milk chocolate
1/4	cup grated chocolate

For the Genoise, break the eggs into bowl, add sugar and mix well. Heat over double boiler, beating vigorously until 113-122° or until the mixture is smooth and foamy. Remove from heat, whip until completely cooled. Mixture should be thick and whitish. Gently fold in sifted flour with spatula, add melted butter. Place in 8" diameter, 2" deep cake mold and cook at 400° for 25 minutes.

For the syrup, mix sugar and water, bring to hard boil. Cook for two or three minutes, then stir in the rum.

For the mousse, melt chocolate over very low heat and set aside. Whisk egg yolks and cocoa over double boiler until mixture is smooth and foamy. Slowly stir in softened butter. Remove from heat, add cool chocolate, stir slowly. If you desire a lighter mousse, fold in stiff whipped cream for more fluffiness.

Cut Genoise in three layers, spreading syrup over each. Put 1/4 of the mousse on the bottom layer, spread evenly. Repeat for the next two layers. Spread remaining mousse mixture on top and sides and garnish with grated chocolate.

Sour Cream Banana Bars

Bars

1 1/2	cups sugar
1	cup dairy sour cream
1/2	cups margarine or butter
2	eggs
1 1/2	cup mashed, ripe bananas, about 3
2	teaspoons vanilla
2	cups flour
1	teaspoon salt
1	teaspoon soda
1/2	cup chopped nuts

Frosting

1/4	cup margarine or butter
2	cup powdered sugar
1	teaspoon vanilla
3	tablespoons milk

For bars: Preheat the oven to 375°. Grease and flour a 15 1/2 by 10 1/2 inch pan. Mix sugar, sour cream, margarine and eggs in a large mixing bowl on low speed for one minute. Beat in mashed bananas and vanilla for 30 seconds. Beat in flour, salt and soda on medium speed for one minute. Stir in nuts. Pour into pan and bake at 375° for 20 to 30 minutes.

For frosting: Heat butter or margarine over medium heat until delicate brown. Remove from heat. Mix in powdered sugar, and beat in vanilla and milk until smooth. Spread on baked bars.

Makes 36 bars.

Blueberry Buckle

3/4	cup sugar
1/4	cup butter or margarine
1	egg, beaten
1/2	cup milk
2	cups sifted flour
2	teaspoons baking powder
1/2	teaspoon salt
2	cups well-drained blueberries, fresh are best

Topping

1/2	cup sugar
1/3	cup flour
1/2	teaspoon cinnamon
1/4	cup butter or margarine

Cream butter and sugar thoroughly. Stir in beaten egg and milk. Sift together flour, baking powder and salt and blend into creamed mixture. Fold in blueberries. Spread batter in greased and floured 9 inch square pan. Combine topping ingredients and sprinkle over batter. Bake at 350° to 45 to 50 minutes or until cake tester comes out clean. Great with coffee or as a snack or dessert.

Pumpkin Squares

1	cup flour
1/2	cup margarine
1	8-ounce package cream cheese
1/2	cup sugar
1	cup Cool Whip
1/2	cup pecans, finely chopped
1	envelope unflavored gelatin
1/4	cup cold water
1	16-ounce can pumpkin
3	egg yolks, beaten
1/2	cup firmly packed brown sugar
1/2	cup milk
1 1/2	teaspoons pumpkin pie spice
1/2	teaspoon salt
3	egg whites
1/4	cup sugar

Mix the flour, margarine and pecans with a pastry blender until crumbly. Pack into a 9 by 13 inch baking dish. Bake at 375° for 15 to 20 minutes until light brown. Cool. With mixer, combine cream cheese, 1/2 cup sugar and whipped topping. Spread on cooled crust and refrigerate. Soften gelatin in water. In a large saucepan, combine the gelatin mixture with pumpkin, egg yolks, brown sugar, milk and seasonings. Cook over medium heat, stirring until the mixture begins to bubble. Cover and cool. Beat egg whites until frothy. Slowly add 1/4 cup sugar and continue beating until stiff. Fold in the pumpkin mixture. Pour over cream cheese mixture and cool until set. Cut into squares and serve with additional topping and chopped pecans if desired.

Makes 10 to 12 servings.

Crunchy Oatmeal Cookies

1	cup shortening
2	cup brown sugar
1	egg
1	teaspoon vanilla
2	cup sifted flour
2	teaspoon baking powder
1	teaspoon soda
3/4	teaspoon salt
1	cup coconut
1 1/2	cups quick rolled oats
3/4	cup chopped nuts
1	16-ounce package semi-sweet chocolate bits

Cream sugar and shortening until fluffy. Add egg, vanilla and beat well. Add flour, which has been sifted with baking powder, baking soda and salt.

Gradually stir in rolled oats, coconut, nuts and chocolate bits. Shape dough into balls the size of a walnut.

Bake on an ungreased cookie sheet 10 to 12 minutes at 375°.

Marcia Adams' Blueberry Frappe

Marcia Adams is host of Marcia Adams' Kitchen

1/2	cup cold buttermilk
1	cup frozen blueberries
1/8	teaspoon almond or vanilla extract
	artificial sweetener to equal 1 tablespoon sugar
	fresh mint or a piece of fruit

Combine all the ingredients in a blender or food processor. Whiz until the mixture is creamy and smooth. Transfer to sherbet glasses or bowls. Serve immediately.

Makes 2 servings.

Peanut Blossoms

1 3/4	cups flour
1/2	cup sugar
1/2	cup brown sugar
1	teaspoon baking soda
1/2	teaspoon salt
1/2	cup solid shortening
1/2	cup peanut butter
2	tablespoons milk
1	teaspoon vanilla
1	egg
	chocolate candy kiss

Combine ingredients in a large mixing bowl. Mix at low speed until dough forms. Shape dough into balls, using a rounded teaspoonful of dough. Roll dough in sugar. Place on ungreased cookie sheet. Bake at 375° 10 to 12 minutes until the golden brown. Remove from oven.

While the cookies are still warm top each cookie with a milk chocolate candy kiss, pressing down so the cookie cracks around the edge.

Baked Alaska Roll

1	boxed angel food cake

Meringue

6	egg whites
3/8	teaspoon cream of tartar
10	tablespoons granulated sugar

For cake: Mix cake batter according to box instructions. Line a jelly roll pan with waxed paper and pour angel food cake batter into pan. Bake at 350° for 15 to 20 minutes or until lightly browned. Cool until just warm to the touch. Flip cake out onto a towel coated with powdered sugar and remove from waxed paper. Gently roll cake in the towel. Allow the cake to fully cool while rolled in towel.

When cool, gently unroll the cake from the towel and fill with either sherbet, ice cream or a fresh fruit and whipping cream combination. Reroll seam side down and place on a sheet of foil. Wrap cake completely in foil and freeze. Just before serving remove cake from freezer and unwrap the foil leaving the rolled cake seam side down on the foil.

For meringue: Beat egg whites and cream of tartar until frothy. Add sugar gradually beating until stiff and glossy.

Cover cake completely with meringue. Place in a very hot oven, about 500°, for 3 to 5 minutes or until meringue is delicately brown. Slip cake onto serving dish.

Note: To save leftovers, rewrap loosely in foil and store in freezer.

Mud Hens

1/2	cup shortening, part butter
1	cup sugar
1	whole egg
2	eggs, separated
1 1/2	cups flour
1	cup miniature marshmallows
1	cup semi-sweet chocolate
1	cup packed brown sugar
1	tablespoon baking powder
1/2	teaspoon salt
1	cup chopped nuts

Cream shortening and sugar. Beat in whole egg and 2 egg yolks. Sift flour, baking powder and salt together. Combine 2 mixtures. Blend thoroughly. Spread batter in a 9 by 13 inch pan. Sprinkle with nuts, chocolate chips and marshmallows. Beat egg whites stiff and fold in brown sugar. Spread over the top of cake. Bake for 20 to 40 minutes at 325°. Cut in squares.

Makes 38 servings.

Delicious Zucchini Bars

Bars

3/4	cup margarine
1	cup brown sugar
2	eggs
1	teaspoon vanilla
1 3/4	cups flour
1	teaspoon cinnamon
1 1/2	teaspoons baking powder
2	cups shredded zucchini
1	cup coconut
1	cup raisins

Frosting

1	cup powdered sugar
2 1/2	tablespoons milk
1 1/2	tablespoons melted butter
1	teaspoon vanilla
1/2	teaspoon cinnamon

For bars: Cream the margarine and sugar until fluffy. Add the eggs, and stir in the vanilla. Sift the flour, cinnamon and baking powder together. Mix well. Stir in the zucchini, coconut and raisins. Spread the batter in a well greased jelly roll pan. Bake at 350° for 35 to 40 minutes.

For frosting: Mix together ingredients. Top bars, cut them, and watch them disappear.

Chocolate Cake

Cake

3/4	cup butter
1/2	cup Drostes cocoa
1 1/2	cups sugar
3	eggs separated
2 1/4	cups sifted cake flour
3	teaspoons baking powder
1	cup water

Frosting

3	egg whites
1 1/2	cups sifted powder sugar
3/4	cup soft butter
1/3	cup Drostes cocoa
1/2	teaspoons cocoa
2 1/2	tablespoons flour

For cake: Soften the butter, cream it, and add sugar. Cream. Add cocoa and beat until light. Beat in egg yolks one at a time. Sift flour. Measure. Sift again with baking powder. Add alternately flour and water to the creamed mixture. Start and end with flour. Fold in stiffly beaten egg whites. Bake in 2 greased 9 inch pans at 325° for 30 to 35 minutes.

For frosting: Beat egg whites to soft peaks gradually adding 3/4 cup powdered sugar until stiff white peaks form. Set aside. Use large bowl and same beaters, and beat the butter until creamy. Separately mix the remainder of the sugar with cocoa and flour. Gradually beat into butter. Fold in meringue and vanilla until well blended.

Cracker Jack

How Cracker Jack Got It's Name: A big hit at the 1893 Chicago World's Fair was a molasses-coated popcorn and peanut confection, scooped out of a barrel.

The creator of this confection, F.W. Ruedkheim, a German immigrant, hadn't given his product a name. The story varies, but in 1896 a salesman tasted the delicacy, smacked his lips and announced, "Now that's a crackerjack." The name stuck.

Later that year, Cracker Jack appeared packaged in individual boxes that sold for a nickel. The price didn't change for more than a half a century.

In 1912, people began finding prizes in their Cracker Jack packages, a tradition that is considered as American as apple pie and, well, popcorn.

1	cup mild molasses
1	cup brown sugar
2	cups white sugar
1/2	cup water
2	tablespoons butter
1	teaspoon baking soda
1	teaspoon hot water
4	quarts popcorn

Boil molasses, sugars and water until hard ball stage. Add butter, baking soda and hot water. Stir and pour over popcorn. Cool and store.

Creme Caramel

Caramel

3/4	cup granulated sugar
1/2	cup cold water

Custard

1 3/4	cups milk
4	eggs, lightly beaten
1/4	cup superfine sugar

To make the caramel: place the granulated sugar and water into a large jug. Microwave on full power for 9 to 11 minutes, or until a golden caramel results. Swirl the caramel evenly around the inside of a suitable, lightly-greased two-pint dish. Leave to set.

Put the milk into a large, clean jug and microwave on full power for 2 minutes. Add the beaten eggs and superfine sugar. Strain onto the set caramel. Cover with plastic wrap and pierce. Stand the dish in a large container, which will act as a water bath. Pour in sufficient boiling water to come halfway up the sides of the dish containing the creme caramel. Microwave on power 5, or simmer, for about 15 minutes or until the custard has set. Remove fromt the water bath. Carefully peel away the plastic and allow to cool. Chill until ready to serve. Turn out and serve very cold with whipped cream.

Charlie Falkenberg's Family Lebkucken

A Christmas Favorite for 4 Generations

1	cup molasses
1	cup brown sugar
1	cup shortening
4 to 5	cups flour
1	teaspoon baking soda
1	teaspoon cloves
1	teaspoon allspice
1	cup hot water
1	cup nuts, preferably walnuts
1	cup raisins
	confectioners' icing
	colored sugars

Beat together the molasses, brown sugar and shortening. Sift together the flour, baking, cloves and allspice and add to the mixture alternately with the hot water. Stir in the nuts and raisins.

Spread the dough into 2-13 by 9 inch pans. Bake at 325° for approximately 30 to 45 minutes. Test, as you would cookies, according to your oven. Frost with confectioners' icing. Sprinkle with colored sugar. While the cookies are still warm, cut them into rectangles.

Lady Baltimore Cake
Wolcott House, Maumee
See Page 152

Double Chocolate Cookies

1	8-ounce package Philadelphia cream cheese
1/3	cup sugar
1	cup or 6 ounces chocolate chips
3	eggs
2	squares bitter chocolate
1/2	cup margarine
3/4	cup hot water
2	cups sugar
2	cups flour
1/2	cup sour cream
1/2	teaspoon salt
1	teaspoon baking soda

Mix the sugar, cream cheese and chocolate chips together and melt in a saucepan over hot water. Remove from heat, then add 1 egg. Set aside. In another double boiler, melt together the margarine and chocolate in the 3/4 cup hot water. To the ingredients in the second mix, add the flour, sugar, salt, 2 eggs, sour cream and baking soda.

Butter and flour a 15 by 10 inch high-sided cookie sheet. Pour the second mixture into the pan. Spread evenly. Spoon the first mixture into the pan by dropping, not spreading. Gently drag the spoon through the mixture, long side to long side. Do not mix well. The dough will look spotty.

Bake at 375° for 30 minutes.

Cool well before cutting into squares.

Makes 20 to 25 bars.

Apple Rolls

1	stick margarine
1/2	cup sugar
1	heaping tablespoon cinnamon
1 3/4	cups sugar
2	cups water
1 1/2	cups tart medium apples, finely chopped, peel and core first
2	cups biscuit mix

Let margarine come to room temperature. Combine sugar and cinnamon, and set aside. Combine in a 9-inch square pan the 1 3/4 cups sugar and water. Place on low heat to get hot while preparing the other part.

In a mixing bowl, combine biscuit mix with just enough liquid to make an easily rolled dough. Roll dough on well-floured surface into a rectangle or circle 1/4 to 1/2 inch thick. Spread dough liberally with soft margarine. Sprinkle the sugar/cinnamon mixture on it. Next spread chopped apples evenly over the surface. Roll like a jelly roll and cut into 1 1/2 inch thick slices. Place cut side down in the hot sugar syrup in baking pan. Bake at 350° for 25 to 30 minutes until golden brown. A sauce forms underneath the rolls.

Serve hot, warm or cold with plain milk, cream, ice cream, whipped topping or lemon sauce.

Russian Creme

3/4	cup sugar
1	package unflavored gelatin
1/2	cup water
1	cup whipping cream, un-whipped
1 1/2	cups sour cream
1	teaspoon vanilla
	fresh raspberries or strawberries

Blend sugar and gelatin in pan. Add water. Mix well. Let stand 5 minutes. Bring to a rolling boil while stirring. Remove from heat and add whipping cream. Mix sour cream and vanilla together, and gradually add the hot sugar mixture. Pour into individual dessert dishes. Chill 4 hours or overnight. Serve with fresh raspberries or strawberries.

Makes 8 half cup servings.

Angel Cherry Delight

12	ounces Philadelphia cream cheese
1/4	cup milk
1	large box angel food cake mix
2	21-ounce cans cherry pie filling
2	12-ounce cartons Creamy Cool Whip

In a small bowl, allow the cream cheese to soften. Add the milk and mix well. In a larger bowl, break cake into bite-sized pieces. Combine cream cheese mixture with the cake. Gently fold in the Cool Whip. Spread contents into an 8 by 11 inch cake pan. Cover with cherry pie filling. Chill for at least 4 hours in a refrigerator. Note: For the Christmas season, add a spoon of mint jelly on each serving to give Christmas color.

Makes 10 servings.

Sour Cherry Dessert

1	cup sugar
1	cup flour
1	teaspoon flour
1/2	teaspoon salt
1	egg, beaten
2	cups canned sour cherries

Topping

1/2	cup brown sugar
2	tablespoons margarine, melted
1/2	cup walnuts, chopped

Mix together sugar, flour, soda, salt and eggs. Add drained sour cherries. Spread in a 8 inch square pan. Mix the topping ingredients and spread on top. Bake for 1 hour at 350°. May be served with whipped topping.

Makes 6 servings.

Manor House at Wildwood, Sylvania

Individually Baked Salmon Lasagna
with Tomato Basil Butter Sauce
by Chef Stephen Brownson
Stephen's Restaurant
629 West South Boundary
Perrysburg, Ohio 43551
See Page 51

Chocolate Zucchini Brownies

1/3	cup margarine
1	egg
1	cup brown sugar
1	tablespoon cocoa
1/2	teaspoon vanilla
1	cup flour
1/2	teaspoon baking powder
1	teaspoon baking soda
1/2	teaspoon salt
1	cup grated zucchini
1/3	cup chocolate chips
1	tablespoon chocolate syrup

Combine margarine, egg and brown sugar in an electric mixer. Add cocoa, vanilla, flour, baking power, baking soda, salt and zucchini. Mix well. Add chocolate chips and syrup. Blend completely. Spread in an ungreased 9 by 9 inch square pan, or the recipe can be doubled to fill a 9 by 13 inch pan. Bake for 30 minutes at 325°. For an extra treat, frost with chocolate icing.

Makes 8 servings.

Cheese Cake

Cake

3	eggs, well beaten
2	8-ounce packages cream cheese, softened
1	cup sugar
1/4	teaspoon salt
2	teaspoon vanilla
3	cups dairy sour cream

Crust

2 1/4	cups fine graham cracker crumbs
1/2	cup melted butter
1/4	cup chopped nuts (optional)
1/2	teaspoon cinnamon

For crust: Combine the graham cracker crumbs with the melted butter, nuts and cinnamon, and press into a spring-form pan 2 1/2 inches deep on sides and bottom. Trim with reserved crumbs.

For cake: Combine the eggs, cream cheese, sugar, salt and vanilla. Beat until smooth. Blend in sour cream. Pour into graham cracker crust. Trim with reserved crumbs. Bake at 375° for 40 minutes or until it has just set. Cool to room temperature, then chill well.

Rhubarb Custard Pie

3	eggs
3	tablespoons milk
1 1/3	cups sugar
4	tablespoons flour
1/4	teaspoon cinnamon
1	teaspoon vanilla
4	cups rhubarb, washed and cut into 2 inch pieces
2	tablespoons butter
	milk/sugar for pie top
2	pie crusts

Beat the eggs, milk, sugar, flour, cinnamon and vanilla in a large bowl until well blended. Stir in rhubarb. Pour into a pie shell, dab with butter, and cover with pie dough. Brush pastry with milk and sprinkle with sugar. Bake at 350° for 1 hour.

Bread Pudding

3/4	loaf bread
3	cups milk
3	eggs
1 1/2	cups sugar
2	teaspoons baking powder
1	tablespoon vanilla
1	teaspoon nutmeg
1	teaspoon cinnamon
1/4	teaspoon salt
1/2	stick butter
1/2	cup raisins

Make sure bread is shredded. Mix all ingredients together until it is in batter form. Bake in greased 9 1/2 by 11 inch pan at 325° for about 65 minutes. Mixture should be crusty on top and moist in the middle. Cut into squares.

Makes 10 servings.

Andersons' Grain Elevators,
Maumee

Miami and Erie Canal, Grand Rapids

Pecan Praline Roll-ups

1	cup firmly packed brown sugar
2/3-1	cup chopped pecans
1/3	cup maple syrup
1/4	cup butter or margarine, melted
8	ounces cream cheese at room temperature
3	tablespoons butter or margarine
1/4	cup confectioners' sugar
2	10-ounce packages Hungry Jack biscuits

Preheat the oven to 350°, and grease a 9 by 13 inch pan. Combine the first 4 ingredients in a small sauce pan. Bring to a boil and pour into 9 by 13 inch pan. Blend cream cheese, butter and sugar until smooth. Separate 20 biscuits. On a floured surface, roll into 4-inch circles. Spoon 1 tablespoon of the mixture on each circle and roll-up. Put seam side down in the syrup mix in pan, about 10 to each row. Bake for 20 to 30 minutes until golden. Cool for about 3 minutes and flip onto serving pan. Can refrigerate before baking, but either bring to room temperature before baking or bake longer.

Makes 10 to 20 servings.

Orange Juice Apple Pie

4 to 6	large Jonathan apples, sliced into thick slices
1	cup sugar
1/2	cup orange juice
1	stick butter or margarine
1/8	teaspoon salt
1	tablespoon flour
2	9-inch pastry shells

Place sliced apples, salt, 1/2 cup sugar, orange juice and butter or margarine in a medium saucepan. Cook apples only until transparent. Mix 1/2 cup sugar and flour together well and add apples. Cook just a few minutes more, taking care so that the apples do not become mushy. Put apple mixture in uncooked pastry shell. Put top pastry shell over apples. Crimp edges of pastry shells together with a fork or fingers. Cut 2 to 3 slits in the top of the shell to allow steam to escape. Bake in a 350° oven until the crust is brown.

Inexpensive Fruit Cake

1	pound raisins
1	cup butter or margarine
1 1/2	cups sugar
3	eggs
3	cups flour
1	teaspoon cinnamon
1	cup walnut meats
1	teaspoon vanilla
1	teaspoon baking soda

Cook raisins with enough water to cover and cook down to 1 cup of juice; drain and let cool. Cream butter and sugar and a half cup of raisin juice. Add well-beaten eggs. Flavor flour with cinnamon and sift three times. Pour nuts and raisins into flavored flour, and mix well before pouring into wet mixture.

Add 1 teaspoon of vanilla. Mix 1 teaspoon soda with rest of raisin juice and add to mixture. Pour into well-greased and floured ring pan or bundt pan. Bake at 350° until brown and tooth pick comes out clean.

Makes 8 to 10 servings.

Norwegian Apple Pie

	vegetable oil spray
2	egg whites or egg substitute equivalent to 1 egg
3/4	cup sugar
1	teaspoon vanilla extract
1	teaspoon baking powder
1/2	cup all-purpose flour
1/2	cup unsalted dry roasted walnuts
1	cup diced apples

Preheat oven to 350°.

Lightly spray an 8-inch pie plate with vegetable oil. Beat the egg, sugar, vanilla extract and baking powder together in a large mixing bowl until smooth and fluffy. Beat in flour until smooth and well blended. Stir in walnuts and apples. Turn into prepared pie plate and bake 30 minutes. Pie will puff up as it cooks, then collapse as it cools. Serve warm.

Serves 8.

Aunt Lee's Chocolate Toto Cookies

6	cups flour
2	cups sugar
1 1/2	cups cocoa
2	heaping teaspoons baking powder
1	teaspoon vanilla
1	teaspoon lemon extract
1/2	heaping teaspoon baking soda
1	teaspoon cloves
1	teaspoon nutmeg
1	teaspoon cinnamon
1	teaspoon allspice
1/2	cup oil
1	cup Crisco
2	cups milk

Sift dry ingredients together. Blend Crisco. Mix wet ingredients and blend with rest. Roll dough into small balls, place on cookie sheet. Bake 15 minutes in a 350° preheated oven. Cover with your favorite icing.

Crane Creek Bird Migratory

Veal Tenderloin Firenze with Risotto
by Chef Matthew Weston
Matthew's Creative Cuisine
4400 Heatherdowns Blvd.
Toledo, Ohio 43614
See Page 87

Cooking Terms

Bake
To cook in an oven with dry heat. Oven should always be preheated 10-15 minutes.

Baste
To moisten foods during cooking with pan drippings or a special sauce, adding flavor and preventing drying.

Batter
A thin mixture of liquid usually including flour, liquid and other ingredients.

Beat
To make a mixture smooth by adding air by a stirring or whipping motion using a spoon or wisk.

Blanch
To immerse briefly in boiling water and cooling quickly in ice water.

Braise
To cook slowly with a small amount of liquid in a tightly covered pan.

Butterfly
To split items such as steak or shrimp through the center without completely separating, and then spreading the sections to resemble a butterfly.

Caramelize
To heat sugar until it is melted and brown, thereby achieving a distinctive flavor.

Candy
To cook in sugar or syrup, and apply to carrots or sweet potatoes.

Clarify
To make broth, butter or stock clear by filtering.

Coddle
To cook in water just below the boiling point.

Cream
To combine two or more ingredients by beating until light and well blended.

Crimp
Sealing the edges of two layers of dough with the tines of a fork.

Dash
Less than 1/8 measuring teaspoonful.

Dollop
To add a small amount, such as a spoonful of a semi liquid as a garnish.

Dot
To distribute small amounts of butter evenly over the surface of dough or pie filling.

Dust
To sprinkle lightly with flour or sugar.

Fillet
To cut fish or meat into pieces without bones.

Flute
To make a decorative scalloped edge on pastry or pie crust.

Glaze
To coat with a thin icing, jelly or liquid either before or after food is cooked.

Knead
To work dough with hands until it becomes smooth and stretchy. This is usually done on a floured surface by pressing, turning and squeezing the dough.

Packed Brown Sugar
Brown sugar pressed into a measuring cup with a spoon. Sugar will hold its shape when cup is inverted.

Partially set
Gelatin mixture that has thickened to the consistency of unbeaten egg whites.

Poach
To cook food in barely boiling water. Eggs and fish are commonly poached.

Simmer
To cook in liquid just below the boiling point. Bubbles form slowly just below the surface.

Soft Peaks
Egg whites or cream beaten to the stage where mixture forms soft rounded peaks when beaters are removed.

Steam
To cook food in a metal basket set over boiling water.

Stir-Fry
To cook cut-up food in a small amount of very hot oil over a high heat. The food should be lifted and stirred constantly as it cooks.

Toss
To mix ingredients lightly with a lifting motion. Pasta and salads are tossed.

Whip
To beat rapidly with an electric mixer or wire whisk. Whipping adds air to a mixture and makes it light and fluffy.

A Guide To Seasonings

Use the following suggestions as a guide when using seasonings. Start with 1/4 teaspoon for each 4 servings; then add more to taste. When substituting fresh herbs for dried, use three times more fresh than dried. Snip fresh herbs or crush dried herbs before using.

Allspice
egg dishes, desserts, fruits, meat dishes, vegetables.

Anise
beef, beets, carrots, cakes, cookies, mixed vegetable salads, pork.

Basil
breads, egg dishes, dips, broiled and roasted meats, poultry, stews, egg dishes, pastas, vegetables, stewed fruits.

Bay leaf
corned beef, stews, fish, bean dishes, potatoes, rice, salads, gravies, marinades.

Caraway
meat loaf, pot roast, stew, poultry egg dishes, fish stews, breads, egg dishes, sauces and spreads.

Cardamom
breads, dressings, fruit salads, meats, poultry, fish.

Cayenne (red pepper)
cream soups, French dressing, Mexican dishes, spreads.

Chervil
egg dishes, dressings, fish, poultry, roasted meats, salads, veggies.

Chili Powder
dips, egg dishes ,French dressing, fish, meats, poultry, vegetables.

Cinnamon
beverages, boiled beef, stewed chicken, barbecue sauce, pastries, puddings.

Cloves
cookies, fruit salads, dressings , marinades, vegetables, pork and lamb.

Coriander
artichokes, bean dishes, curries, fruit salads , gingerbread, pork stew, roast poultry, pastries.

Curry Powder
beef sauces, cheese spreads, creamed vegetables dips, egg dishes, fruit compotes, seafood, rice, beef, lamb, pork, poultry.

Dill (weed, seed)
beef, breads egg dishes ,dressings , lamb, fish, poultry, seafood.

Fennel
breads, egg dishes , dressings , meat roasts, stews, fish, poultry.

Ginger
breads, cookies, desserts, fruit, marinades, meats, poultry, salad dressings, vegetables.

Marjoram
breads, egg dishes, gravies, roasted meats, poultry & meat pies, seafood, salads, vegetables.

Mace
cakes, cookies, chowders, fondue, fish and veal dishes.

Nutmeg
cookies, desserts, egg dishes, fruits, pastries, sauces.

Rosemary
breads, casseroles, fish, roasted meat & poultry pies, fish, stews, and vegetables.

Saffron
breads, cakes, casseroles, fish stews, rice, seafood salads.

Tarragon
casseroles, dressings, fish, roasted meats & poultry, salads, vegetables.

Thyme
breads, egg dishes, meat loaf, poultry pie, seafood, salads, vegetables.

Turmeric
curries, dips, pickles, relishes.

Farmers'
Market, Toledo

Emergency Substitutions

If You Don't Have	You Can Substitute
A tablespoon of cornstarch (for thickening)	2 tablespoons of all-purpose flour.
1 package active dry yeast	1 cake of compressed yeast.
1 teaspoon baking powder	1/4 teaspoon baking soda plus 1/2 cup buttermilk or sour milk (to replace 1/2 cup of liquid called for).
1 cup of cake flour	1 cup minus 2 tablespoons all-purpose flour.
1 cup of buttermilk	1 tablespoon lemon juice or vinegar plus just enough whole milk to make 1 cup then let stand for 5 minutes.
1 cup of whole milk	1/2 cup of evaporated milk plus 1/2 cup of water or 1 cup reconstituted nonfat dry milk.
1 cup of light cream	2 tablespoons butter plus 1 cup minus 2 tablespoons whole milk.
1 cup of whipping cream, whipped	2 cups whipped dessert topping.
1 cup of corn syrup	1 cup granulated sugar plus 1/4 cup liquid.
1 cup of honey	1 1/4 cups granulated sugar plus 1/4 cup liquid.
1 cup granulated sugar	1 cup packed brown sugar or 2 cups sifted powdered sugar.
1 egg	In most cases use 2 egg yolks.
2 cups of tomato sauce	3/4 cup tomato paste plus 1 cup of water.
1 cup of tomato juice	1/2 cup tomato sauce plus 1/2 cup of water.
1 clove of garlic	1/8 teaspoon garlic powder.
1 small onion	1 teaspoon of onion powder or 1 tablespoon of rehydrated minced dried onion.

Index of Recipes

Lucas County Courthouse

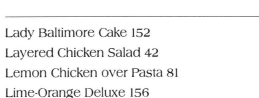

Scalloped Potatoes with Carrots and Onions 121
Schnitz Soup 27
Seafood Caper Pasta 60
Shrimp & Scallop Sauté with Lobster Dill Sauce 54
Shrimp Sauce 130
Smoked Turkey Linguine 67
Snickerdoodles 160
Sour Cherry Dessert 179
Sour Cream Apple Pie 167
Sour Cream Banana Bars 170
South Wales Cakes 164
Spaghetti with Chicken Tomato Sauce 75
Special French Toast 147
Spicy Fried Cabbage 115
Spinach Enchiladas 124
Steamed Custard 26
Stewed Tomato Casserole 106
Stroganoff 87
Stromboli 98
Stuffed Eggplant 121
Stuffed Spaghetti Squash 102
Stuffed Summer Zucchini 120
Sugared Asparagus 106
Summer Casserole 124
Summer Chicken 70
Summer Rice Salad 34
Sunburst Stir-Fry 75
Sweet Hot Fish Sauce 138
Sweet Pepper Salad 32
Swiss Ham Ring-Around 97

Taboule Salad 34
Taco Beef Soup 29
Taco Salad 38
Tangy Cucumber Ring 106
Tangy Low-Fat Ranch Dressing 47
Tennessee Parsnip Soup 29
Texas Hush Puppies 147
Thai Curry 79
Three-Bean Salad 41

Tokyo Chicken 79
Tomatoes Rockefeller 104
Tortilla Roll-ups 12
Trout in Parsley Chive Sauce 134
Turkey Barbecue 74
Turkey Stuffed Baked Peppers with Raisins 102
Turkey Vegetable Soup 27
Turnip Souffle 107

Veal Shank 89
Veal Tenderloin Firenze with Risotto 87
Vegetable Dip 135
Vegetable Pancakes 119
Vegetable Pie 109
Vegetable Sandwich 120

Walnut Yogurt Ring 160
Winter Salad Lunch 44
World's Easiest Zucchini Bread 148
Wort Bread 148

Zebra Cake 161
Zucchini Bars 174
Zucchini Pie 113123
Zucchini Pizza 118
Zweiback 152

Contributors

Marcia Adams

Fran Anderson

Mary Jo Anderson

Amy A. Avers

Joann Backlund

Elizabeth Barry

Brian Bennett

Fifi Berry

Bob Bevec

Marie Bianco

Todd Biggs

Ellen Black

Carol Block

Clara M. Bloomer

Dee Blumer

John Bodner

Rosemary Bone

Raye Ann Boroff

Cynthia Crosby Bowland

Grace Boyd

Joanne Brell

Barbara J. Brengartner

Sharree K. Brenneman

Valerie Brighton

Ann Broderick

Benjamin Brown

Stephen C. Brownson

Ellie Brunner

Walter A. Churchill

Joanne Colby

Joe Crea

Wanda Crosby

Rose Dandar

Dawn M. Dempsey

Julie Doll

Helen Duffy

Judith Hauman Dye

Sharon Emch

Mary Ann Esposito

Mary L. Falcone

Faye Fenwick

Amy Finkbeiner

Sandy Flick

Cheryl Tyler-Folsom

Pat Frechette

Liz Freriks

Susan M. Fulkerson

Louise Gallant

Carol Geracioti

Christopher D. Glass

Judy Gonia

Druscilla Griffin

Bob and Emily Guion

Esther Grubb

Gregory Gullo

Letty Haigh

Goldie Hall

Florence Hartenfelt

Beatrice Hartung

Margaret Hiett

Ann Jane Hileman

Margaret Hilfinger

George Hirsch

Bridget Brell Holt

Patricia Holz

J.P. Hornyak

Nancy Horton

Anne Humphrey

Kate Jackson

Kathy Jarret

Leslie Jobe´

Marge Johns

Cher Johnson

Kris Johnson

George A. Kamilaris

Marcy Kaptur

Irene Kaufman

Marilyn Kelley

Annie Lee Kennedy

Carol Kerekes

Linda S. Kerul

Peter V. Knapper, Sr.

Robbie Ward Knapper

James Koehl

Martin Kokotaylo

Kathleen Kozy

Mary Kreinbrink

Susan Kurdys

Ruth C. LaFrance

Nancy A. Lapp

Carla Laver

Yvette Levin

Patrick Lewandowski

Margaret Linehan

Judith Lodes

Christine Lowery

Kleia R. Luckner

Kathy Magliochetti

Frances Mancini

Mary Mancini

Mildred A. Mannik

Anne G. Marquis

Marcene Marsa

Helen McMaster

Thomas O. Meyer

Linda Milewski

John D. Mihaly

Alvetta Moore

Shelly Moore

Betty Moran

Elizabeth A. Morrison

Gloria Moulopoulos

Olivia Murphy

Kevin Navarre

Leonard Nelson

Donna Niehous

Frieda L. Nofziger

Charlie B. Nunn

Marion Nunn

Sheila Odesky

R. Andrew Odum

Carol Orser

Sister Ann Felicitas Peplin OP

Jacques Pepin

Suzanne M. Petti

Colleen Pickering

Deirdre Pierce

L.Z. Pippert

Mary Alice Powell

Carolyn Putney

Marna Ramnath

Nancy Ravin

Susan Reams

Tabaitha Reams

LaNelle Rhodes

Barbara Richards

Mary Richter

Denise Riedel

Beau Rochte

Geneva D. Rodgers

Joan Roe

Marsh Rorick

Nancy Rudolph

Alice Ward Russell

Jane Ruvolo

Mona S. Sayed

Karen Schaefer

Sister Rose Schaller

Alice Seeburger

Dawn Shuler

Kay Silk

Margarete Simon

Brooke Simonds

Nancy Slattery

Anna L. Smith

Dorothy Greer Smith

Genevieve Smith

Jeff Smith

Bethanne Snodgrass

Vickie Souder

Heather Speck

Jeanne Connors Spooner

David Steadman

Kathy Steadman

Maryellen Stein

Nick Stellino

Eileen Stranahan

Karen Szymanski

Gretchen Taylor

Mary H. Thomas

Shirley E. Timonere

Diane Venable

Ethel Walden

Patty Westermeyer

John D. Wesley

Matthew Weston

Sue White

Valencia Whitlow

Martha Williams

Jo Ann Winzeler

Louise Mikesell-Wireman

Sandra Wiseley

Dorothy Young

What's Good To Eat:

The Best of Northwest Ohio

For additional copies of this cookbook, contact:

WGTE TV 30
P.O. Box 30
Toledo, Ohio 43697

or call: (419) 243-3091

The price per copy is $26.57 (includes shipping and tax).